HINDU GODS AND GODDESSES
AN INTRODUCTION

Writer-journalist **Sunanda Verma** was born in Bulgaria, raised in India and Fiji, and nurtured in South Africa and Singapore. Passionate about exploring cultures and finding common threads, she has worked as a TV news producer, made documentary films, authored the Namaste Series of books, co-authored a dictionary and co-edited an index of the *Sriramacharitamanasa*. Discover more at www.sunanda.net

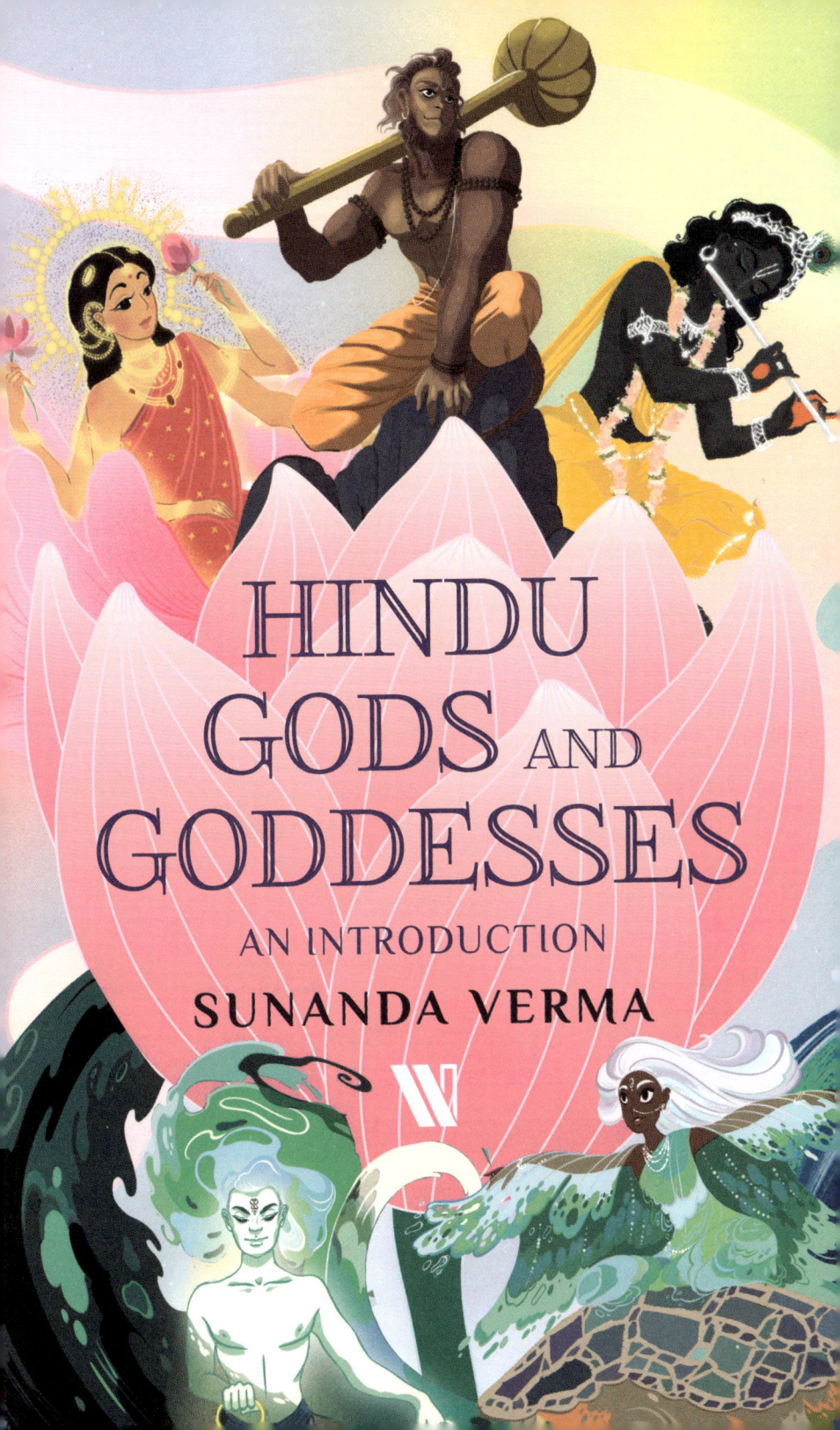

Published by Westland Books, a division of Nasadiya Technologies Private Limited, in 2025

No. 269/2B, First Floor, 'Irai Arul', Vimalraj Street, Nethaji Nagar, Alapakkam Main Road, Maduravoyal, Chennai 600095

Westland, and the Westland logo are the trademarks of Nasadiya Technologies Private Limited, or its affiliates.

Text © Sunanda Verma, 2025
Illustrations © Nasadiya Technologies Private Limited, 2025

Sunanda Verma asserts the moral right to be identified as the author of this work.

ISBN: 9789371972390

10 9 8 7 6 5 4 3 2 1

Book design by Pratik M. Kalekar

The views and opinions expressed in this work are the author's own and the facts are as reported by her, and the publisher is in no way liable for the same.

All rights reserved

Printed at Nutech Print Services, India

No part of this book may be reproduced, or stored in a retrieval system, or transmitted in any form or by any means, electronic, mechanical, photocopying, recording, or otherwise, without express written permission of the publisher.

To Anshuman,
for his love of stories.

CONTENTS

NAMASTE 9

PRAKRITI / NATURE
Dyaus 17
Prithvi 19

Agni 23
Vayu 29
Varuna 35
Indra 39
Kubera 47
Ishaan 51
Nirrti 53
Yama 55

Navagraha
Surya 51
Chandra 65
Mangal~Budha~Brihaspati~Shukra~Shani~
Rahu~Ketu 69

PURUSH / LIVING BEINGS

Shakti / Energy **77**
Saraswati 79
Lakshmi 83
    Sita 89
    Radha 93
Parvati 97
    Durga 101
    Kali 107

Ganga 109
Yamuna 115

Trideva / Trinity... **118**
Brahma 119
Vishnu 125
Shiva 131

Kamadeva 135
Kartikeya 139

SAMANVAYA / SYMPHONY
Hanuman (Nara + Vaanara) 145
Ganesha (Nara + Gaja) 149

Dashaavatara (Purush + Prakriti) 154
Matsya 155
Kurma 159
Varaaha 161
Narasimha 163
Vaamana 169
Parashurama 171
Rama 175
Krishna 179
Gautama Buddha 185
Kalki 189

Harihara (Hari + Hara) 191
Ardhanareeshvara (Naari + Nara) 195

Samudramanthana 197
(Deva + Daanava, Visha + Amrita)

GLOSSARY 202
SELECT READING 205
ACKNOWLEDGEMENTS 206

NAMASTE

The word 'namaste' means 'I bow to the divine in you', suggesting that God exists in both you and me.

This book is about Hindu gods and goddesses. Think of the ones you know. What do they look like? Aren't they all so different? Some look like humans, some like animals and some are half-human, half-animal. Some have long hair, others short hair, or no hair at all. They may be gigantic or as small as dwarves. They live in the sky, on tall mountains, in deep seas or far beneath the earth. Just like the vast, diverse land that imagined them, our gods and goddesses look, think and act differently. They have different powers and their own ways of solving problems. They experience ups and downs and emotions—from jealousy and pride to compassion and empathy. Everything from nature (e.g. rain, Indra) to disease (e.g. measles, Sheetala Mata) is seen as a god or goddess.

Are you a number person and want to know exactly how many gods and goddesses there are in the Hindu religion? Well, there are said to be 330,000,000 of them!

The number is a metaphor for our numerous gods and goddesses. For example, if someone has four heads, it means that they have the intelligence and knowledge of four people!

Many gods have many names, many stories and many versions of those stories. Some even have many lives. There are infinite ways to interpret their thoughts and actions. You'll see some of them in this book and many others around you. For instance, in trees, Krishna is associated with the peepul or sacred fig.

Hinduism has no single founder, no one god and no single holy book. Its interpretations are limitless. Individuals can choose whom to worship, how to pray, and which customs and rituals to follow. A mountain, a stone, a tree, a plant, or even an earthen pot can be worshipped.

At its core, Hinduism is about the worship of diverse ideas and concepts. That is why it is often described as a way of life or a code of behaviour—Sanatana Dharma—which means eternal law or virtues, rather than a religion.

People first worshipped elements of prakriti (nature) because they could see and feel them.

Elements like fire, rain, sun, wind, and water were turned into gods and given human traits. Their gifts were valued and their powers feared. Agni, the fire god, was imagined with a crackling voice! Next came purusha (living beings). Shakti, or energy, was recognised as the force behind all action. Women, with the power to create life, were seen as the embodiment of Shakti.

Three essential powers were personified as goddesses: Saraswati (knowledge), Lakshmi (wealth) and Parvati (strength). These goddesses were then paired with male deities who supported their roles—Brahma with Saraswati (creation needs wisdom), Vishnu with Lakshmi (wealth sustains life), and Shiva with Parvati (destruction for renewal requires power).

All these (and other) gods and goddesses have unique features that make them special. The number of hands they have indicate their strength. The objects they hold in their hands represent their powers and abilities. They also have animals as their vaahana (vehicles), which shows that even gods and pashu (animals) work together and need each other. This idea of friendship and camaraderie between humans and animals is rather literally embodied by Hanuman, the vaanar god. The concept of *samanvaya*, or harmony among seemingly different elements, is a key part of the Hindu way of life. This dynamic between prakriti (nature) and purusha (living beings), maanava (humans) and pashu (animals) and naari and nara (the female and male principles) is explored in a number of ways in the Hindu mythos, as we will see, in concepts such as the Dashaavatara, in gods such as Ganesha and Ardhanareeshvara, as well as in events like the Samudramanthana (churning of the ocean).

The roles of gods and goddesses evolved over time, adapting to changes in society while maintaining continuity.

The earliest documentation of these deities is found in the Vedas, the oldest being the *Rig Veda*. The word 'Veda' comes from the root 'vid', meaning 'to know'. The Vedas, believed to be about 3,500 years old, form the foundation of Hindu tradition. They are hymns in Sanskrit offering guidance—not rules—on rituals, worship, pilgrimage, and daily life. Passed down orally with strict rules of rhythm and pronunciation, they were eventually written down. These are *shruti* texts, meaning 'that which was heard' by rishis, who taught them orally. The Vedas have no single author. The sage Vyasa is considered the compiler of the four Vedas:*Rig Veda, Yajur Veda, Sama Veda* and *Atharva Veda*. In contrast, *smriti* texts are based on memory and attributed to specific authors. Unlike shruti, which is divinely heard and more authoritative, smriti literature expands on and interprets Vedic ideas. The Ramayana and Mahabharata are epics that fall under the smriti category. They include stories of creation, destruction, kings, sages, gods, cosmology, geography and moral philosophy. These epics guide us on how to live well, be kind and seek harmony.

This book is a fun and engaging way to learn about popular Vedic and Puranic gods. The following pages contain stories from ancient texts such as the Ramayana, Mahabharata and folk traditions across India. You'll learn about each deity's attributes and the temples and festivals dedicated to them. Keep in mind that their depictions vary depending on artists, cultural traditions and regions. This book focuses on the qualities, symbols and values they represent—not just how they look. What makes this book special is how it connects mythology to our lives today.

Though there are countless stories of gods and goddesses, they all point towards a life of peace or contentment—interpreted variously as bliss, truth or ultimate consciousness. When is the mind at peace? When you've spoken the truth, done no wrong, been fair, helped someone, shown kindness, remained calm, sought solutions and acted responsibly. Living in this way leads to godhood, moksha or the realisation that there is no separation between you and the divine. Just as there are many gods and goddesses, there are many paths to truth. 'The truth is one, the wise call it by many names' (*Rigveda* 1.164.46).

Hinduism also believes in rebirth. We are born based on the karma (actions) of our past lives, and what we do now will shape our next one. That's why your everyday choices matter so much.

Hindu philosophy is about exploring and recognising the inherent divinity within you and outside you. This is what I hope this book will help you do.

LEGEND

 direction

 weapon

 temple

 festival

 colour

 vehicle

 grain/legume/seed

 stone

Throughout the book, you'll notice symbols next to the descriptions of each god and goddess. These indicate their direction, weapon, temple, associated festivals, vehicle, grain and sacred stone.

PRAKRITI
NATURE

Prakriti means nature in Sanskrit and is considered divine. Respect for nature emphasises living in harmony with our environment.

Dyaus and Prithvi are the eternally young creators and preservers who gave shape and form to the entire universe. They are thus the eternal parents of all beings—including the gods. They are wise, righteous, energetic and generous with gifts to their children.

Dyaus is Aakaasha, the sky father, and Prithvi is the earth mother. Dyaus is often imagined as a mighty bull, and Prithvi as a nurturing cow.

DYAUS
Ether

Dyaus, the god of ether, is subtle, strong, broad and vast. He grants food, wealth and fame, and is known for his wisdom and righteousness. He supports and protects all his children equally. Boundless and present in every atom, Dyaus carries the winds and sounds, delivering messages in the sky about what is to come. He smiles through the clouds.

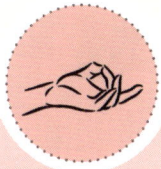

In Yoga, the Aakaasha mudra is a hand gesture that helps balance the space element and helps heal sinus, hearing and throat issues.

It is Aakaasha (ether) that enables the stability of Prithvi (earth), the flow of Varuna (water), the passion of Agni (fire), and the lightness of Vayu (air). The stillness of Aakaasha makes all movement—and therefore life—possible.

Did you know?

Aakaasha resides in your body—in your sinus cavity, ear canals, stomach, lungs and bone joints.

PRITHVI
EARTH

PRAKRITI

Prithvi is adorned with oceans, rivers, streams and the mountains are her bosom. Ever patient, giving and forgiving, she holds wealth in her womb (think of where metals and minerals come from). She is tawny, black (the colour of soil), has dark knees and is covered with rocks, forests, trees, shrubs, herbs and more. Her fragrance is unique and has entered every being.

> Ittar (perfume) makers in Kannauj, Uttar Pradesh have been creating mitti ittar, which is said to be the scent of rain on parched earth for hundreds of years!

Her bosom is golden (when Indra showers abundantly, the ripe grains turn golden) and yields grains, vegetables, fruits, crops and medicines. She nourishes her children with everything; she is nature. She is creative, compassionate, merciful and fertile. She births a variety of life forms, from bipeds, quadrupeds—from the largest reptiles to the tiniest of worms. She is stable and grounded. She sits on a lotus on a golden throne, propped by the King of Nagas (serpents) Shesha. She unifies diverse people who come from different cultures, follow different religions and rituals and speak different languages—but live together in the same home—earth. Prithvi is the protector of the past, present and future. She is loving, truthful, enthusiastic, knowledgeable and kind. She moves fast and trembles when angry.

Did you know?

Bhumi pooja is done on land before beginning construction or farming.

SAVING PRITHVI

Jaya and Vijaya were the formidable and loyal gatekeepers of Vaikuntha, the residence of Vishnu. They were extremely particular about not disturbing Vishnu when he was resting. When the four sons of Brahma came to meet Vishnu, Jaya and Vijaya refused them entry. Not used to being refused, Brahma's sons got so furious that they cursed the guards to be born on earth. Though the gatekeepers cried for forgiveness, and even Vishnu interceded, saying that they were just performing their duty, the curse was irrevocable. And so, Jaya and Vijay were born as Hiranyakashipu and Hiranyaaksha.

Hiranyaaksha's devotion to Brahma was unmatched. He worshipped the god for many, many years. Pleased with such devotion, Brahma granted a boon that made Hiranyaaksha invincible. Hiranyaaksha's intentions were evil, but he wanted the boon before he set forth to wreak havoc. With Brahma's boon, no being, divine or mortal would be able to cause his death.

Thrilled by the boon, Hiranyaaksha now spread his evil upon unsuspecting victims on Earth. He unleashed chaos on the Devas and stormed Indra's celestial palace. Overwhelmed by fear, the Devas fled and hid in secret caverns deep within the earth. Next, Hiranyaaksha took control of Prithvi submerging her into the depths of Paataala Loka, the netherworld. With all life being threatened, Manu and Shatarupa, the parents of all humans, rushed to Brahma seeking his help and support to end the havoc Hiranyaaksha was creating.

But Brahma put his hands up. He said only Vishnu could help. Time was short, Prithvi who sustained all life was in deep distress.

Vishnu took the avatar of a varaaha, a mighty creature whose body was the colour of dark clouds and whose eyes shone like lightning. He had sharp white tusks, the head of boar and the body of a man. This varaaha towered over the landscape like a colossal mountain, piercing the clouds with his tusks and the skies with his thunderous roar. Diving into the depths of the vast ocean, he searched for Prithvi.

Once Hiranyaaksha realised what was happening, his face turned red and his nostrils flared with rage as he charged towards the varaaha. The varaaha plunged his sharp tusks into the depths of the ocean and raised Prithvi up. She gasped for air as she came out exhausted.

Following a fierce confrontation, the varaaha finally put an end to Hiranyaaksha by hurtling him into the sky.

All became quiet, a sense of order returned and Prithvi and all her children breathed again.

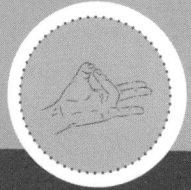

In yoga, the Prithvi mudra is a hand gesture that helps balance the earth element, which resides primarily within tissues, such as skin, hair and bones.

AGNI
GOD OF FIRE

Agni is a messenger between gods and humans, the earth and heavens. He is the son of strength, born of two dry sticks.

Do you see smoke above a flame? That is Agni at work. Your message is on its way, connecting you to the gods above.

Agni is described as a ruddy man reflecting the colour of his glowing flames. His flames are like roaring sea waves. He has two heads, three legs, seven arms, dark eyes and eyebrows, red hair, and a beard. He has seven tongues and flames of fire come from his mouth. Seven streams of glory radiate from his body. He has sharp golden teeth and can eat anything. He has a crackling voice.

He rides a ram and wears a garland of fruits. His face, hair, and back glow with all the ghee that is offered to him. He never grows old, for he is born every day. Gods eat through Agni, and he accompanies them whenever they visit humans. His chariot is named Dhumaketu, after the smoke that trails him wherever he goes. 'Dhumaketu' translates to 'comet'. Agni's chariot moves as fast and is as fiery as a comet! His weapon is the Agneyastra. When released, it shoots flames that cannot be put out by regular ways of extinguishing fire.

Agni is wise, true to his word, the bringer of wealth, light and knowledge. He is always a leader. He is worshipped on every occasion, is a priest at ceremonies, and so knows all the secrets and wishes of humans. He is also a witness: he watches everything. He brings warmth and security and has the power to renew. He loves eating ghee, sesame seeds, barley, rice, honey, yogurt and kheer.

Agni is a guest in every home, he is fair to everyone and hates no one. He accepts all that is offered to him and brings a glow wherever he goes.

No one can live without Agni; all life is with Agni; the body turns cold after death. High above, he is the sun; a little below, he is lightning; and at our level, he is the fire in your belly, in the kitchen, in the altar, in molten lava and in countless other places

You might have noticed that as they make offerings to Agni during a pooja, people utter the word 'swaahaa'. This is because after Agni married Swaahaa, he declared that he would accept offerings only after her name was taken. And so, to ensure their prayers are received by the gods (remember, Agni mediates between heaven and earth), people say 'swaahaa'. Brahma, in fact gave Agni the power to purify whatever went through him (think of boiled water). Agni was also the second-most important god among the Vedic Gods and appears in 200 hymns in the *Rig Veda*. The *Rig Veda* begins by invoking Agni.

 The geometric symbol of Agni is a triangle pointing upwards.

HINDU GODS AND GODDESSES

THE DAY AGNI HID

When Puloma was a little girl, she did not want to get to bed on time. Her parents told her why it was important, but she would not listen. As a last resort her father would say, 'Puloma, if you don't sleep now, the asura Puloman will come to take you and I will not stop him.' Scared of the asura, she would immediately close her eyes and fall asleep within seconds. However, the asura Puloman thought Puloma's father was serious. He became convinced that Puloma's father really thought that Puloma and Puloman would make a good couple and that one day they would marry and live happily.

Puloman lost track of her over the years but he did not forget her. He knew she had married a rishi called Bhrigu.

One day, as Puloman passed by a hermitage nestled deep in the woods, he spotted a woman who looked a lot like Puloma. (It was indeed her, the girl of his dreams. Now grown up, Puloma had become the wife of rishi Bhrigu, and the two were expecting a baby.)

He wanted to find out if it was Puloma, but she and the rishi, who must be her husband, were always together. So when Puloman learnt that the rishi had to leave for work and that his wife had stayed back home, he jumped at the opportunity. He laughed out aloud and went to their cottage.

Puloma was a gracious host. She was just as he thought she would be, but he needed to be sure that it was indeed her. The asura knew that Agni lived in every home, so he went to find the fire god. 'Is my host Puloma, the same little girl who slept only after her father took my name every night? Is she the wife of rishi Bhrigu? Speak the truth or I will curse you, Agni,' he thundered.

Agni is a witness; he knows everything because he sees everything. At this moment he did not know what to do. If he spoke the truth, Puloma would be in trouble, if he lied, he would be in trouble.

Caught between duty and fear, Agni revealed the truth. Overjoyed, the asura took the form of a wild boar, intending to take Puloma on his back and run away. In the commotion, Puloma's baby fell out of her womb. The sky lit up with lightning that very instant, and the asura was burnt to ashes as he turned to look at the baby.

Clutching her newborn son, Puloma fled from the chaos, her tears forming a river that trailed behind her.

Bhrigu returned to a family in panic and distress. 'Who revealed your identity to the asura? He could not have figured it out by himself.'

The rishi's eyes blazed with anger when he learnt it was Agni. 'From this moment you will be omnivorous, you will eat anything and everything, including garbage,' he cursed.

'How can you curse me? I was only doing my duty as the witness!' Agni defended himself, hurt by the injustice.

He retreated from the world and went into hiding, leaving the gods, sages and ordinary people in despair. Without Agni, nothing could be done. Desperate, the gods and sages went to Brahma for help.

Brahma calmed Agni's fury. He said that from now on, whatever Agni ate would be purified. Grateful for Brahma's words and wisdom, Agni resumed his duties, bringing light and warmth to the world.

Did you know?

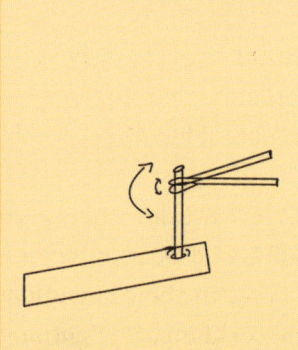

- The ritual of *agnimanthana* (fire churning) is performed using two wooden sticks for all yagnas—where prayers and offerings are made before a fire. Fire is born from the vigorous 'churning'—manthana—of two sticks perpendicular to each other. The churning motion creates friction, which creates sparks. These sparks are placed on a bed of dried cow dung cakes as kindling to start a fire. The yagna is then performed using that fire.

VAYU
GOD OF WIND

Vayu is the wind god. He provides us with the air we breathe. You can hear him, you can feel him, but you can never see him!

Vayu is a strong, young, handsome man with white skin (reflecting the speed at which he moves). His palace is called Gandhavati and he lives in Vayuloka.

Vayu holds a white flag in his right-hand, which flutters about as he moves noisily in his shining chariot. His chariot has a golden seat and is drawn by a pair or red or purple horses. Depending on the need, his chariot can be drawn by 99, 100 or even a 1000 horses (storms need a lot more horsepower than a light breeze). When not in his stunning chariot he goes about on a deer holding his white flag.

Vayu is the swiftest of gods, as swift as thought! He can go anywhere and everywhere. He is playful and loves playing with leaves, making trees rustle and dance. He is always travelling. He is a purifier and messenger as he carries fragrances of flowers, aromas, odours and even the whispers of secrets.

Vayu is the producer of sound.

In yoga, the Vayu mudra is a hand gesture that helps regulate the Vayu element within the body.

Can you think of some musical instruments that exist because of Vayu? They produce sound by the vibration of air within instruments, such as the bansuri, shehnai, algoza, nadaswaram, been/pungi, pepa and harmonium.

Vayu is powerful, never rests and is present everywhere. He can also be violent and bring destruction. Vayu moves touching the sky, turning it orangish red as dust clouds blow on earth. Vayu is good friends with the god of rain, Indra, and the two often travel together. They both like to drink Soma, the energizing divine drink.

> Wind power is a clean and renewable energy source. Windmills use the power of wind and can produce electricity, grind grain or even pump water with it!

There is no life without Vayu, because no one can live without breathing or air. He is the life force and the energy that keeps us alive.

Vayu is generous and kind and gives equally. He has healing powers and gifts good health and a clear mind. Ever noticed how refreshed you feel after a run or a walk in fresh clean air?

> You are Vayu when you share kindness and love equally, and when you give 'breathing space'!

Did you know?

Vayu won the race for the first draught of Soma, and at Indra's request, shared a quarter of it with him.

VAYU, THE FATHER

King Dasharatha of Ayodhya and his three wives, Sumitra, Kaushalya and Kaikeyi, held a yagna. They were conducting special prayers to have children.

At the same time, in a thick, beautiful forest, Anjana was praying to Shiva. She and her husband Kesari, a Vaanara chieftain, longed for a child, too.

Moved by Anjana's devotion, Shiva appeared, smiled and said, 'Your wish will be fulfilled!'

Meanwhile, as the yagna progressed in Ayodhya, Agni appeared with a ladle of kheer and gave it to Dasharatha, saying, 'Give this to your wives to share and eat. Your wish will be fulfilled.'

Overjoyed, Dasharatha divided the kheer equally between Sumitra, Kaushalya and Kaikeyi.

Just as the queens were about to eat their kheer, a big kite swooped down and snatched Sumitra's portion from her hands. It happened in a flash! When they recovered from the shock, Kaushalya and Kaikeyi shared half of their portions with Sumitra. Months later, Kaushalya gave birth to Rama, Kaikeyi to Bharata, and Sumitra to Lakshmana and Shatrughna.

Meanwhile the kite was flying over the forest where Anjana and Kesari were staying. Spotting a more attractive feast crawling near a big tree, the kite let go of the kheer. Vayu swiftly scooped up the kheer before it could touch the ground and carried it into the palms of Anjana, who sat deep in prayer. Kheer had never tasted so good, thought Anjana, as she licked the last traces of it. Months later, Anjana gave birth to Aanjaneya, who was later also known as Hanuman.

Since Vayu brought the kheer to Anjana, he is also known as Aanjaneya's father. Vayu protects Aanjaneya like a father, too.

When Aanjaneya was a toddler, he leapt at the rising Surya (sun), mistaking it for a ripe fruit that he could eat! When Surya realized Aanjaneya's intention, he got nervous and cried for help. Indra responded to Surya's cries and was so annoyed at seeing a little vaanara wanting to gobble up Surya that he struck him with his weapon, the vajra (thunderbolt). The blow to his jaw landed little Aanjaneya on earth with such a loud thud that Vayu came to see what had happened. Upset at seeing him injured, Vayu vanished, taking Aanjaneya along.

With Vayu gone, all air disappeared. No one could breathe. Life became impossible. The gods rushed to Brahma. Brahma was furious at the impatience and actions of Indra. But what good is anger in a time of crisis? Brahma, Indra and all the other gods rushed to Paataala Loka, where Vayu sat nursing Aanjaneya's wound.

Brahma healed Aanjaneya while Indra apologized profusely. Everyone earnestly pleaded with Vayu, 'Please, for everyone's sake, return!'

'I am not going anywhere without Aanjaneya,' Vayu was firm.

'From now on, no weapon can injure Aanjaneya,' Brahma declared.

'He will be a Chiranjeevi, an immortal,' Indra declared. 'My vajra hurt his hanu (chin), and so he will also be known as the valiant Hanuman.'

'Please return, for everyone's sake, Vayu!' they all requested in unison.

After some convincing, Vayu returned with Hanuman. There was a sigh of relief.

VARUNA
GOD OF SKY, OCEANS AND WATER

Varuna is young and white, reflecting the colours of the foamy waves of the ocean. He sits on a makara (crocodile) and holds a paasha (noose) and kalasha (pitcher) in his hands. He ensures that law and order is maintained.

Varuna lives in a house with a thousand doors built by Vishwakarma, the divine architect. In the centre is a grand canal of pure water. In his court around him sit Samudra, Ganga and other river gods and goddesses.

He has a thousand eyes and very good eyesight, so he can always see those who reach out to him. The thousand doors in his house allow anyone to walk in and seek help. He is mighty, can be scary and is the ruler of the universe.

It is he who has made the depths of the sea and made channels of rivers. They flow at his command. The moon and the stars move by his will. The stars are his eyes and oversee the actions of people.

He oversees law and punishes those who make mistakes but have no remorse and forgives those who accept their mistakes and learn from them.

Varuna is wise and helps truth grow and accomplish all big tasks by truth. No life can exist without Varuna. He is generous. He gives people salt and fish and asks for nothing in return.

Did you know?

 A downward-pointing triangle is the symbol of water in sacred geometry.

VARUNA, THE RESCUER

Ravana was on his way to Lanka carrying a Kaamalinga (the linga that fulfilled all desires). This stone linga granted the worshipper all their desires. Ravana, a great devotee of Shiva had requested the god to move to Lanka. Shiva, however, was not willing to move to Lanka himself. He gave Ravana the Kaamalinga instead, saying that it would be as good as Shiva being in Lanka when it reached there. However, if the Kaamalinga touched the ground anywhere en route, it would have to remain there.

When the other gods saw Ravana with the Kaamalinga they were concerned. If Ravana began fulfilling his wishes, the gods would be in big trouble. They got together to find a solution. After long hours of discussions, they agreed that only Varuna could help. Varuna would need to enter Ravana's belly.

Meanwhile, Ravana walked excitedly towards Lanka, thinking of all the wishes he would have fulfilled once the Kaamalinga, which he carried on his head with care and reverence, reached his kingdom.

What happens when you drink a lot of water? You need to pee. That is just what happened to Ravana as Varuna entered the king's body. Ravana's bladder was full. He was desperate to relieve himself, but he did not want to, because he would have to keep the Kaamalinga down. At the very same moment, Indra, the king of gods, appeared disguised as an old man. Ravana quickly asked the old man if he could hold on to the Kaamalinga while he relieved himself. The old man said he could hold it for an hour but no longer. Ravana handed him the Kaamalinga and dashed off to relieve himself, saying he would be back in less than half that time!

An hour passed, then another, another and then yet another. It had been four hours, and Ravana was still not done relieving himself. Indra had waited for a long time, then finally called out to Ravana that he could not hold the Kaamalinga any longer. When Ravana was finally done, he found the Kaamalinga placed on the ground. He tried his best to pick it up and continue to Lanka, but it would not budge.

This spot is said to be in Deoghar, in Jharkhand, where the linga is worshipped at the Baba Baidyanath Temple.

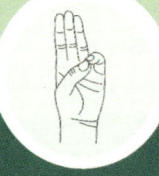

In yoga, the Varun mudra is a hand gesture that helps regulate the water element within the body.

INDRA
GOD OF RAIN, THUNDER AND LIGHTNING

Indra is the king of gods, who lives in Svarga.
When it rains, when you see lightning flash across the dark skies or you hear the rumble of thunder, know that Indra is at work! It means that Indra is in a fight with demons who keep trying to steal cows from Svarga!

The rainbow you see in the sky is the Indradhanusha, Indra's dhanusha or bow. Indra is as vast as the earth. He is a man with a thousand eyes all over his body. He has a long neck, a strong jaw and four strong arms. He rides a white elephant with four tusks called Airavata. This divine animal emerged during Samudramanthana (churning of the ocean) and is the king of elephants. The king of gods rides the king of elephants! Indra helps his worshippers, is generous and brings peace and prosperity. He fights the demons of droughts and darkness. His weapon, the vajra, a thunderbolt, pierces through clouds that hold water and brings relief to parched lands. It is Indra who ensures that rivers flow full of water, that harvests are bountiful and that there is enough to eat. He shapes mountains such that rivers flow and streams reach everywhere.

Vajraasana, the thunderbolt pose in yoga, represents power, strength and stability. It is a kneeling pose and the only asana that can be performed after meals.

Indra is a master of every weapon used in warfare. People ask for his help and support with special weapons.

Indra loves Soma, a drink loved by the gods and made with the leaves and stalks of the Soma plant. He loves it so much that he instinctively gravitates towards the rhythmic sound of the Soma leaves being pounded. Sometimes when he has had too much, he agrees to everything his worshippers ask for! He brings the Soma plant from heaven to earth.

Indra is strong and brave, but his temper and arrogance often get the better of him. When they are in check, he is formidable.

Did you know?

Indra is the most popular deity in the *Rig Veda*. Almost one-fourth of the text glorifies him!

Read the story of the Samudramanthan on Page 197

PROUD INDRA LEARNS A LESSON

Indra was a god quick to be pleased and as quick to get upset. He liked to feel important and powerful and loved it when he was praised.

On earth, the people of Vrindavan worked hard. Their livelihood depended on agriculture and that depended on good rains. Only if it rained at the right time and in the right amount would their hard work bear fruit. Indra thus played an important role in their lives. Abundant showers meant prosperity, while drought brought hardship. In years of plenty, the villagers would joyously worship Indra and express gratitude for his generosity. In times of scarcity, they would beseech him for mercy and seek forgiveness for any transgressions.

One fateful year, the rains poured blessings, and Vrindavan transformed into a lush green paradise. In gratitude, the villagers planned a grand festival to honour Indra. They got busy with preparations, cleaning, cooking and decorating Vrindavan with flowers and lights. Little Krishna woke up after his afternoon nap to a bustling and bedecked Vrindavan. He asked his father what the fuss was all about. The festival was in honour of Indra for his kindness and rain. More importantly, it was so that Indra continued to be happy with them and ensure good weather and rains, his father replied.

Krishna laughed. 'It isn't Indra who makes it happen, it's your own hard work. If no one works hard in the fields or takes care of the cows, even Indra cannot help. You should be working hard, not praying to please Indra.'

Krishna's words made sense to the villagers, who put their energy into work instead of celebrating Indra.

But Indra was so enraged that he unleashed his fury upon Vrindavan, commanding torrents of rain and thunderstorms to ravage the land. It poured and poured and poured even more. The villagers did not know what to do. They went to Krishna. Krishna smiled and lifted the colossal Govardhan mountain and balanced it on the little finger of his left hand. Now a huge umbrella resting on Krishna's finger, it sheltered and protected everyone who lived in Vrindavan from Indra's fury.

For seven days, the villagers stayed beneath the protective shadow of the Govardhan, shielded from the deluge.

Indra couldn't believe what he saw. As his pride and arrogance crumbled, he came to understand that true strength lies not in power but in humility.

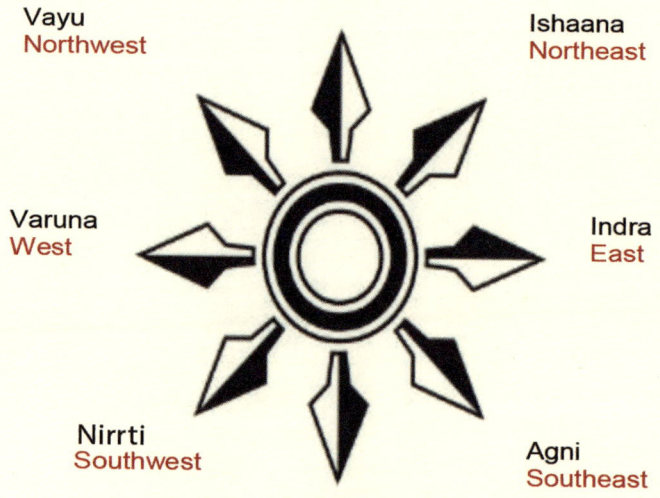

ASHTADIKPAALAS
THE EIGHT GUARDIANS OF THE DIRECTIONS

Dikpaalas are guardians who protect and look after the eight directions. Indra, Agni, Varuna, Vayu (who you have read about), along with Kubera, Ishana, Nirrti and Yama are the Ashtadikpaalas. They are often depicted on the walls or ceilings of temples.

The Khajuraho temples in Madhya Pradesh, for instance, have the Ashtadikpaalas guarding the eight directions of the complex.

Did you know?

In ancient times when rituals or yajnas were performed, offerings were made to each Dikpala to harmonise the space and also mind, body and universe.

 North

 Gada

 Kuber Bhandari Temple in Karnali, Gujarat

 Dhanteras, Akshay Tritiya

KUBERA
GOD OF RICHES

Kubera is the treasurer of the gods. He looks after all treasures that lie below the earth—gold, silver, diamonds, rubies, gems and minerals. He distributes and guards all wealth. He is the dikpaala of the north.

He is a dwarf with three legs, a twisted torso, eight teeth and a big belly. He wears a lot of jewellery and carries a bag of gold coins. He is often depicted with a mongoose on his lap that spits out gems whenever it opens its mouth.

Kubera rides a vehicle drawn by men and so is called naravaahana. He also has a magnificent self-propelling aerial vehicle called Pushpak, gifted by Brahma. Its golden windows are decorated with precious gems. It has seats and even beds!

He leads a life of opulence and abundance beyond imagination. His garden, called Chaitratha, is a place of joy. There is no sorrow, suffering, fear, death, anxiety or hunger. People are in excellent health and live here for up to 12,000 years.

Kubera is responsible for ensuring abundance and the responsible use of wealth.

PRAKRITI/ ASHTADIKPAALA

Did you know?

Vishnu took a huge loan from Kubera and is at Tirupati Balaji (also known as Shree Venkateshwara Temple) because he is repaying the loan.

KUBERA'S FEAST

Kubera lived a life of plenty. Why wouldn't he—he was the god of riches! A huge house studded with gold and diamonds, flowing silk, luxurious furnishings, the most beautiful garden with scented water fountains, finest of foods—he had it all. Kubera knew he had a lot more than most and wanted to show off. He thought the easiest way to do that was to organize a feast at home.

Anything to do with Kubera was lavish, so he planned an elaborate meal, ordering the most flavourful vegetables and fruits and engaging the most talented chefs from near and far. He had a long guest list because he wanted everyone to be talking about his house, his grand lifestyle and his unparalleled hospitality.

First on his list was Shiva. Shiva had given Kubera the boon of never diminishing wealth. Kubera went to invite the family personally. He was immediately struck by the bare simplicity of their house. A god with great powers but no shimmering gold or sparkling diamonds around him? Kubera felt a bit sorry for Shiva and a lot vainer about his wealth.

'I want to invite you for a feast at my house,' said Kubera to Shiva and Parvati.

'What are you celebrating?' asked Parvati.

'I am celebrating … um … um … celebrating life,' said Kubera, covering up his true intentions.

Shiva and Parvati looked at each other and smiled. They knew why Kubera was organizing the feast.

'We will not be able to come, Kubera, but little Ganesha can represent us at your "celebration of life,"' said Shiva.

Though Kubera was disappointed that Shiva and Parvati could not come, he was grateful that little Ganesha would. He hoped that Ganesha would talk about his gorgeous house and opulent lifestyle back at home.

Little Ganesha had a big appetite and arrived on time for the party. Kubera was thrilled to see him. Ganesha would be able to taste all the five hundred dishes that were specially prepared for the feast and talk about it too!

Ganesha wasted no time and sat down to eat. The gold pots, plates and cutlery added to the glitz. Ganesha seemed to finish as quickly as he was served. A battery of people ran from the kitchen to the table and back to refill his plate. The food frenzy got people in the kitchen worked up too. The pots and pots of food prepared to feed thousands of guests were now running empty. They couldn't cook as fast as he was eating! Kubera arranged for food from neighbouring cities, but that wasn't enough either.

Little Ganesha looked up from his empty plate towards Kubera, 'Is that all you have? I am hungry.'

Kubera turned red with embarrassment.

Little Ganesha left for home. Kubera followed him.

'He didn't have enough food; I am still hungry.' said Ganesha to Shiva and Parvati.

Kubera stood behind Ganesha, embarrassed.

'I underestimated Ganesha's appetite,' said Kubera.

Parvati gave little Ganesha a fistful of plain puffed rice in a coconut shell.

Ganesha ate that and smiled broadly. 'Ma, this was so nice, I am so full!'

 Vrishabha

 Northeast

ISHAANA
LORD OF THE NORTHEAST

Ishaana is a form of Shiva. He is the directing lord of the northeast direction.

He has three eyes and two hands and holds a trishula (trident) and a kapaala (skull). He has a calm disposition and crystal-like brilliance and translucence. He wears white and sits on a tiger skin. He has a jata mukuta (top bun) and on it sits the crescent moon. He rides a bull.

He is youthful, powerful and the master of knowledge.

Kubera, associated with wealth, resides in the north; Indra, associated with knowledge resides in the east. Situated between the two, Ishana represents the coming together of wealth and knowledge.

Ishaana is the source of spontaneous, limitless, boundless grace for all beings and in every world. He is associated with Aakaasha (ether) and looks upwards.

Southwest

NIRRTI
GODDESS OF DARKNESS

Nirrti is the goddess of darkness and represents destruction, untimely death, corruption, calamity and sorrow. She is the dikpaala of the southwest.

She is dark skinned, has two hands and in them holds a sword and a severed head, and often depicted as standing over a prostrate body. She wears dark clothes, and her messenger is the crow.

She is the wife of Adharma (unrighteousness) and the mother of sons Bhaya (fear), Mahabhaya (great fear) and Mrityu (death). Nirrti is also associated with poverty, hunger and infertility. She brings with her dark aspects and so is prayed to be driven away.

Her realm has no light or warmth; it is an endless, dark, decaying pit meant for those who act against the basic ideals of society. Nirrti, however, safeguards those born into crime, if they are ethical.

	Mahisha		South
	Paasha		Dharamraj temple in Bharmour, Himachal Pradesh

YAMA
GOD OF THE DEAD

Yama is the god of the dead. The first being to ever die, he discovered the way to the other world. He guides all those who die and takes them to his kingdom and gives them a safe, comfortable home. His work is about justice, accountability and the cycle of birth and death. He is the dikpaala of the south.

Yama is the son of Agni and Sanjana (also known as Sharanya) and the twin brother of Yami (Yamuna).

He is a handsome, strong, cheerful man and the king of deceased ancestors. In his kingdom, loved ones reunite with their friends and family. He gifts bright homes to those who have lived a righteous life of truth and kindness.

He lives in Pitraloka.

He has two dogs with four eyes each and wide nostrils. They guard the entrance of his kingdom and move among people as messengers. Crows and pigeons are his messengers as well.

Yama is the lord of justice, that is why he is also called Dharmaraja. In this work he is assisted by Chitragupta, who keeps complete records of the good and bad deeds of humans in their life on earth. Upon their death, these records of their karma are pulled out to decide if they will be reborn as superior or inferior beings in their next life. Yama makes the final decision based on these records.

THE PRICE OF PRIDE

Yama knew he was handsome. He liked looking good and put effort into it. 'What a handsome god of death!' he would exclaim each time he gazed into a mirror.

There came a time when all Yama did was admire himself in the mirror. His work began to suffer. His messengers would come to him, but Yama would ignore them. Chitragupta had all the records ready, but Yama did not make any judgements. There was no space on earth, not enough water and food, but Yama remained busy admiring himself and hosting lavish parties.

Shiva was not amused. He took his work seriously and expected everyone to do their work with sincerity too. He summoned Yama to Mount Kailasa, where he lived.

Yama knew that Shiva had called him over because he was doing everything other than his work. He was guilty and did not know what to expect. But Shiva welcomed him with a broad, warm smile. Yama wasn't sure what was going on, because Shiva was known for taking serious action against those found guilty. He was grateful to have been saved from Shiva's wrath. He counted his blessings!

'Good to see you, Yama,' said Shiva, 'Do you mind getting me some water from the river?'

'That would be my absolute pleasure,' said Yama, jumping at the opportunity of doing something for Shiva. He took Shiva's water pot and walked with a swing in his steps to the river! Just as he was filling the pot, he saw a frightening face in the river staring back at him. It was green with bulging, bloodshot eyes, a big moustache and two large, curved horns on the head!

He was so scared that he couldn't even scream. He got back on his feet and ran back as fast as he could. Panting, breathless and shaken from what he saw, Yama narrated the events to Shiva.

Shiva listened calmly and then smiled. 'Touch your head, Yama,' he said.

Yama put his hand on his head. He felt something hard and curved. Oh no! They were the horns of the man in the river! So, was what he saw in the river his own reflection?

Yama pleaded and begged Shiva to return him his looks, but Shiva closed his eyes, a smile on his lips.

Yama ran with folded hands and bowed head to Brahma and then to Vishnu, but neither helped.

'You must face your karma. You did not perform your duty and this is its result,' said Vishnu.

Yama knew Vishnu was right. Yama's own work was about judgement on karma.

'However, what I can do for you is remove those horns and put them on your new vaahana (vehicle),' said Vishnu.

'Vaahana?'

Yama looked up to see a buffalo with two curved horns standing beside him.

Since then, Yama has taken his work seriously, and is seen as a green man dressed in red. He has large bloodshot eyes, a black moustache, a crown and a flower in his hair. He holds a danda (staff), a mace and a paasha, and rides a buffalo.

Surya (Sun)

Chandra (Moon)

Mangal (Mars)

Budha (Mercury)

Brihaspati (Jupiter)

Shukra (Venus)

Shani (Saturn)

Rahu

Ketu

NAVAGRAHA
NINE GODS OF ASTRAL POWER

The Navagraha are the nine gods of Hindu astrology. They include the guru of devas, Brihaspati; the asuras Rahu, Ketu and even their guru Shukracharya besides Surya, Chandra, Mangala, Budha and Shani. Each of these has unique characteristics, colours, vaahanas, as well as their preferred plants or plant parts and gemstones.

Most temples have the Navagraha grouped together. There are also Navagraha temple clusters which have nine separate temples dedicated to each of these nine heavenly bodies.

 Navagraha mandir, Guwahati, Assam

 Konark Sun Temple in Konark, Odisha; Modhera temple in Modhera, Gujarat; Martanda Temple in Anantnag, Kashmir

 Suryaastra

 Makara Shankranti, Pongal, Chhath

 Yellow

 Horse

 Wheat

 Ruby

SURYA
SUN GOD

NAVAGRAHA

Surya, the sun god is the light of life and wisdom.
This radiant god is a ruddy man reflecting the colour of his energy and heat. He has three eyes and four arms. His eyes, hands and tongue are golden. Light radiates from him, and when he stretches his arms to bless, energy and inspiration flow to all those around him. He sits on a red lotus. He rides a golden chariot drawn by seven white-footed horses that represent the seven days of the week and the seven colours that together make white light!

His weapon is the Suryaastra, which discharges fire and has many sharpened edges and spinning wheels. It produces a dazzling light that dispels darkness and can dry up sources of water.

Surya is the son of heaven and is seen every day. He banishes darkness and makes life possible on earth by bringing warmth and light. Surya is always awake and is constantly on the move. He is generous and brings light to all on planet earth.

He governs time. Our day begins when he brings daylight and ends when he leaves.

Surya stands for truth, is far sighted, keeps his promises (rises every day). He travels from the east (sunrise) to the west (sunset) every day like a swift red bird.

He is the source of life and energy (think of solar power) and motivates people into action. He gives knowledge, success and

Did you know?
The Gayatri mantra is dedicated to Surya, the Sun God.

good health (Vitamin D, for instance). He is a symbol of power and is literally the energy that sustains life on earth.

It is because of him that seeds turn to plants and we have fruits and trees.

> The sun is the heart of our solar system. It the largest object in it, and its gravity holds the planets and other celestial bodies together. Its interactions with the Earth change seasons, ocean currents and the climate.

Surya brings warmth, light and positivity into the world around.

Even the days of the week are dedicated to the first seven of the navagrahas, and this is reflected across many languages and cultures across India and the world. For instance, Sunday is called Ravivaar, Ravi being another Sanskrit (and Hindi) word for sun, and vaara meaning day. In yoga, the right nostril, called surya nadi (sun channel), is associated with the qualities of the sun-strength, energy and efficiency. Breathing in and out through the right nostril is believed to energise and help focus.

The surya namaskar or sun salutation in Yoga is a sequence of asanas honouring the energy and vitality of Surya.

WHEN SURYA'S BRIGHTNESS BECAME A PROBLEM

The radiant Surya faced an unusual problem—his own brilliance. His wife Sanjana (also called Sharanya) found his radiance too intense to bear, struggling to even look at him! When she could bear it no more, Sanjana went to her father's home.

Surya felt completely broken. He wanted to be with Sanjana, but his own radiance was the problem. He asked his father-in-law for help. Vishwakarma, the architect, engineer and design specialist of the gods, was known for his ideas and creativity. He agreed to shave off some of Surya's brilliance. With skilful precision, he reduced Surya's radiance by one-eighth, ensuring that it remained bright and potent for Surya, yet tolerable for his daughter.

Looking at the shimmering shavings of Surya's lustre—though a mere fraction of his radiance, they were extremely powerful and fiery—he got an idea. And that is how the formidable Sudarshana Chakra, the discus wielded by Vishnu; the mighty Trishula, Shiva's trident; the gleaming swift vela, the spear of Kartikeya, were created. They were made from Surya's brilliance and Vishwakarma's own creative genius!

Vishwakarma's engineering and creativity brought Surya and Sanjana together, while making the cosmos richer with divine tools for its protection and preservation.

> Aditya, Anshu, Anshuman, Avi, Bhanu, Bhaskar, Mihir, Prabhakar, Ravi, Rohit, Savita, Savitri or Sunoor are all names of the Sun.

CHANDRA
MOON GOD

NAVAGRAHA

Chandra is the light of the night and the celestial timekeeper. This luminous god is the lord of all vegetation.

He is fair complexioned, wears white, sits on a lotus and moves swiftly and gracefully on his white chariot which is pulled by ten white horses across the sky. The handsome god has rounded features, big beautiful sparkling eyes and a charming smile that wins people's hearts immediately. He has two hands and holds a gada and a lotus in them. He wears a gold crown and a pearl necklace. He speaks softly in a melodious tone. His vaahana is an antelope. He is calm and cool, and his favourite grain is rice.

Chandra is peaceful, affectionate and nurturing. He is Lakshmi's brother; they came out of Samudramanthana. He is a true romantic at heart and is married to the 27 nakshatras (lunar mansions).

He is also called Soma, after the most valuable plant in the Vedic times.

Chandra represents recurrence, repetition, rhythm and inspires expression in poetry and other creative activities. He rules moods and emotions and brings fertility.

A full moon suggests enlightenment and success, a waxing and waning moon suggest the ups and downs of every action.

> Even though the Sun and the Moon appear similar in size from earth, the moon is about 400 times smaller than the sun. It is also 400 times closer to the Earth!

Read the story of the Samudramanthan on Page 197

CHANDRA AND HIS UPS AND DOWNS

Chandra had twenty-seven wives. They were all daughters of Daksha. Though initially hesitant, Daksha had agreed to them marrying Chandra so long as the moon god promised to love and care for all of them equally.

Chandra had agreed, but soon after one of them became his favourite. Her name was Rohini. Chandra began to spend most of his time with her, ignoring the others. No one likes being ignored. So when his behaviour started to affect, they went to their father to complain.

Daksha was known to be short-tempered. When he heard from his daughters that Chandra had not kept his word, he became furious. His nostrils flared, his ears turned red, his eyes bulged and he looked ready to burst.

'Your powers and your lustre will decline with each passing day, Chandra, I curse you!' Daksha thundered.

Everything turned quiet as these words left his mouth. It was so quiet that you could hear a flower fall.

His daughters were filled with regret. They went to their father because they thought he would speak to Chandra and get him to mend his ways—they hadn't wanted him to be cursed! Now, one day Chandra would completely disappear! It would become pitch dark. How would the world live like that?

Chandra begged and pleaded, cried and howled for Daksha to take back his curse, but a curse once given cannot be taken back.

'You know that cannot be done, Chandra. I cannot help you,' said Daksha, 'If there is anyone who can, it is Shiva.'

Crestfallen, yet holding on to this sliver of this hope, Chandra went to Prabhas Patan in Gujarat. He established a linga there and prayed to Shiva. Pleased by Chandra's prayers, Shiva appeared, smiled and said, 'I cannot take away the curse, Chandra, but I can reduce it. From today your lustre will increase for 15 days in Shukla Paksha and decrease for 15 days in Krishna Paksha. You will be in your complete radiance on Poornima, the night of the full moon and unseen on Amavasya, on new moon days.'

Chandra was at a loss for words. He could not believe that his lustre would decrease and there would be a day when he would not be seen at all.

Shiva knew what Chandra was thinking. 'Chandra, I will hold you as Ardhachandra, in your crescent form, in my hair. It will remind you of the curse, but it will also remind you and everyone else that I am always with those who remember me, even when they are at their weakest.'

Shiva is known as Somnath, because he took care of Soma. He is also known as Chandrashekhar, because he holds the crescent on his head.

The linga that Soma established and prayed to became the Somnath temple in Gujarat.

MANGAL (MARS)

Mangal is a young warrior who is armed with a spear. He is said to be born when Shiva's sweat dropped on earth!

Red   Ram   Red masoor daal   Red coral

BUDHA (MERCURY)

Budha is the son of Chandra. He is a gentle being, liquid when flowing and solid when stable. Communication is his strong point.

Green   Yali   Green moong   Emerald

BRIHASPATI (JUPITER)

Brihaspati is the guru of the devas. The wisest among the navagrahas, he carries a bow whose string is the basis of dharma.

 Saffron   Elephant   Peanuts, chickpeas   Yellow sapphire

SHUKRA (VENUS)

Shukra is the guru of the asuras. He stands by truth, reality and justice. He is intuitive and creative.

 Diamond white   Dark horse   White beans   Diamond

SHANI (SATURN)

Shani is the son of Surya and the brother of Yama. He is the lord of karma and justice.

Dark blue   Crow   Sesame   Blue sapphire

RAHU

Rahu is represented as a mouth with no body that threatens to swallow the sun or the moon, a metaphor for an eclipse.

Smokey grey   Black lion   Urad daal   Garnet

KETU

Ketu is the sibling of Rahu, represented as a tail without a head, a metaphor for a comet.

Khaki green   Eagle   Horsegram   Cat's eye

12 Jyotirlinga Shrines

- Somnath
- Mallikarjun
- Mahakaleshwar
- Omkareshwar
- Kedarnath
- Bhimshankara
- Kashi Vishwanath
- Trimbakeshwar
- Vaidyanata
- Nageshwara
- Rameshwaram
- Grishneshwar

Did you know?

Jyotirlingas are believed to have manifested themselves or become installed at twelve places in India. Somnath in Prabhas Patan, Gujarat; Mallikarjun in Srisailam, Andhra Pradesh; Mahakaleshwar in Ujjain, Madhya Pradesh; Omkareshwar in Mandhata, Madhya Pradesh; Kedarnath in Uttarakhanda; Bhimshankara in Bhimshankar village in Maharashtra; Kashi Vishwanath in Varanasi, Uttar Pradesh; Trayambakeshvar in Trimbak, Nashik, Maharashtra; Vaidyanata in Chitabhumi, Deoghar, Jharkhanda; Nageshvara in Darukavana, near Dwarka, Gujarat; Rameshwaram in Rameshwaram, Tamil Nadu; Ghushmeshvara also known as Grishneshwar in Verula, near Ellora caves in Maharashtra.

PURUSH
LIVING BEING

Purush means 'all beings', in Sanskrit. In the Hindu philosophy all living beings are considered divine and each carry a unique spark of the same cosmic spirit. Diversity in thought, action, form and behaviour is celebrated. Gods, humans, animals are all seen as sacred and worthy of reverence.

The concept of Purusha varies across different schools of thought, with some seeing it as a personal god, others as an impersonal principle and still others as the individual soul.

SHAKTI
SUPREME ENERGY

Shakti is the primordial, infinite and supreme energy that has been and will continue to be. Shakti means strength or power and is imagined as a woman. Though she cannot be seen, her presence can be felt. She lives in every being and is the power that changes things. She is the ability to do work.

She is present in every movement—from that of your thoughts to that of the earth! She is the energy that turns a seed into a huge tree, which makes living things grow. She carries the idea of possibility and the ability to make it a reality.

She is the feminine energy, the mother goddess, the one who makes creation, sustenance and destruction possible.

In creation, she is Saraswati, the goddess of knowledge. Brahma is her consort. In sustenance, she is Lakshmi, the goddess of prosperity. Vishnu is her consort. In restructuring, she is Parvati, the goddess of recreative energy. Shiva is her consort.

Shakti is the force that destroys demons that we can see and that we cannot see, such as anger, lust, greed, delusion, arrogance and jealousy within us.

You are Shakti. You only have to realise it.

Did you know?

At the Chottanikkara Bhagavathy temple in Kochi (Kerala), Shakti (also known as Rajarajeswari or Adiparasakthi), is worshipped in her three forms thrice a day: Saraswati in the morning, Lakshmi at noon and Durga in the evening.

HINDU GODS AND GODDESSES

SARASWATI
GODDESS OF KNOWLEDGE

Saraswati is the goddess of speech (and thus the vehicle of knowledge), learning and creativity. She is the mother of the Vedas, the one who inspires and illuminates minds.

In the *Rig Veda,* Saraswati is a mighty river, the best among mothers. She nourishes all those who come to her.

The calm elegant goddess is dressed in white reflecting peace, purity, light and knowledge. She is simple and beautiful, suggesting that humility is the real measure of wisdom. She has four arms and holds a book, a mala (rosary), a water pot and a veena in each. She sits on a lotus and rides a hansa (swan) that can separate milk from water (that is, knows truth from lie and real from unreal).

She plays the veena, a stringed musical instrument, and represents the harmony between knowledge and creativity. She fills the universe with melodies that inspire and uplift. She is the mother of swaras and ragas.

Saraswati flows like a river in music, art, debating, writing, researching, learning and is in all tools of knowledge like books and stationery. Schools, universities, libraries and all places of learning are her temples.

She isn't very easy to find; you can find her only when you seek her. She represents clarity of thought and encourages us all to stay curious and keep learning.

She is the shakti of Brahma (there is no creation without knowledge) and has emerged from Brahma's mind as the purest form of knowledge and creativity.

WHEN SARASWATI SAT ON KUMBHAKARANA'S TONGUE

Did you know that once every day Saraswati comes and sits on your tongue and whatever you say in that moment comes true?

Kumbhakarana, Ravana's younger brother was wise, strong and a great warrior. He was huge as a mountain with as huge an appetite.

Kumbhakarana wanted a boon. He decided to pray to Brahma and sat in meditative prayer. Many years passed, but Kumbhakarana's devotion stayed strong. Brahma was pleased with Kumbhkarana and appeared before him.

'Ask what you wish for and it shall be granted,' said Brahma.

While all this was going on, Indra had been feeling uneasy, but didn't know why. But when he saw Kumbhakarana sitting in prayer to Brahma, he understood the reason for his anxiety. Kumbhakarana wanted to take Indra's place and rule the heavens. Ravana's brother had undertaken that meditation for a boon, and Brahma was known to give boons without much thought. Indra was troubled. He thought hard and he thought deep about who he could ask for help.

'Saraswati! The goddess of speech and knowledge is the only one who can help me,' thought Indra. Indra prayed to her in sincerity and in urgency. When the goddess appeared before him, he explained to her the game plan of Kumbhakarana to her and requested do something about it.

Kumbhakarana had waited years for this moment. Just as he began asking for a boon from Brahma, Saraswati sat on his tongue and tied it. He wanted to say 'Indrasana,' which was the seat of Indra, but the words that came out were 'nidrasana,' the state of sleep! Next, he wanted to ask for 'nirdevatvam,' the absence of all gods, but the words he uttered were 'nidraavatam,' continuous sleep!

'Tathaastu, so be it,' said Brahma instantaneously.

With her work done, Saraswati left for her next devotee.

It all went by so quickly that Kumbhakarana took a minute to understand what had happened! Once he realised it, he pleaded with Brahma to take back the boons. But a boon once given cannot be taken back.

This is why Kumbhakarana slept for six months of a year and stayed up to eat for the next six months, year after year.

Did you know?

The word 'veda' signifies knowledge and comes from the root word 'vid', to know. The Vedas were written down centuries after they were composed; until then, they were communicated orally, committed to memory.

The veena is like the great-grandparent of all Indian string instruments. It helped set the rules for music that many other instruments follow.

 Uluka

 Diwali, Lakshmi puja

 Shri Ambabai Temple in Kolhapur, Maharashtra; Ashtalakshmi Temple in Chennai, Tamil Nadu; Sri Mahalakshmi Temple in Goravanahalli Karnataka

LAKSHMI
GODDESS OF WEALTH

Lakshmi is the goddess of wealth, prosperity and abundance. She is radiant, as brilliant as gold and as illustrious as the moon. Her four arms represent the four goals of life: dharma, virtue and duties; artha, wealth; kaama, love; and moksha, self-knowledge. She is dressed in red silken garments, wears fine gold jewellery and has flowers in her hair. She emits a lotus-like fragrance that extends to more than a thousand kilometres. She sits on a lotus and her vaahana is the uluka, an owl, with eyes the shape of gold coins! Two elephants stand by her side showering her with flower petals. They represent hard work, intelligence, loyalty and strength.

Lakshmi is extremely particular about cleanliness and is drawn towards sparkling, homes and clear minds. However, she can leave as quickly as she arrived. To those who please her, she provides resources and wealth, the power of the mind, intellect and moral and ethical qualities. She loves to travel. Often, she goes to places where Saraswati lives (wealth comes to those who have knowledge). Sometimes though she can become the reason for Saraswati to leave (if wealth becomes the reason you argue and quarrel, you can be sure knowledge has left).

She is the daughter of Varuna and the sister of Chandra. She is the Shakti of Vishnu and helps sustain the world. She has great authority and power; Vishnu can grant a wish only when she has approved it. She has been his partner in all his avatars. When Vishnu took the avatar of Vaamana, she was Padma; with Parashurama, she was Dharani; with Krishna, she was Radha; with Rama, she was Sita.

Friday is her day, and she holds a special place for merchants, accountants, businesses and all those in the business of wealth. Lakshmi brings material wealth and teaches the value of inner wealth, of the importance of values such as love, compassion and gratitude. She symbolises being vigilant in the dark, knowledgeable in the face of ignorance and wise or prudent when at a crossroads.

With its keen vision and silent flight, her vaahan symbolises vigilance and wisdom, and the ever-watchful eye of the goddess.

> Lakshmi and Kubera may seem the same, because they are both about wealth and abundance, but remember that Lakshmi is the goddess of abundance and prosperity of all kinds, not just material wealth. Kubera, on the other hand, is associated with material wealth and riches.

> In the Vedas, Lakshmi is called 'Shri'. This is why many people involved in businesses write 'Shri' at the top of their documents dealing with accounts (such as invoices and account sheets) in the belief that she will bless their business with a continuous flow of wealth.

> On the last day of the Rath Yatra, Lakshmi is offered rasgullas in the Jagannatha temple in a ritual called Niladri Bije. The story goes that Lakshmi was unhappy with Jagannatha because he had left her alone at the temple and gone on a nine-day trip with his brother Balaram and sister Subhadra. The goddess was so annoyed that she locked the temple doors and wouldn't let her husband enter. Hoping that it would placate her enough to let him into the temple, Jagannatha got rasgullas for Lakshmi. His plan worked, and Lakshmi accepted his apology.

LAKSHMI AND HER VAAHANA

It was a beautiful evening at Vaikuntha. Lakshmi had just finished her work for the day when she received a message from Vishnu that he would be delayed at work.

'What a lovely evening,' thought Lakshmi. 'Perfect for an evening outing.'

Lakshmi loved going to different places. She did not stay anywhere for long, but she liked visiting people and exploring places. Vishnu's vaahana, Garuda, was always happy to take her wherever she wanted. Today, he wasn't around, and she wished she had her own vaahana.

'All gods have their own vaahana,' thought Lakshmi, 'I think it's time I get my own mount, too.' With those thoughts she set out on a leisurely walk. The trees and flowers made her extremely happy, and she decided that she would take whichever creature she saw first as her vaahana.

Meanwhile, Indra too had left his home for a walk. His 'walk', however, was different: he sat on his elephant, Airavata, who did all the walking! Indra had met Brihaspati, the guru of the gods earlier in the day and hadn't stopped smiling since. Brihaspati had told Indra that he would win Lakshmi's favour like never before today. The goddess would load Indra with so much wealth that he wouldn't need to ask Kubera for anything ever again!

The possibility of meeting Lakshmi excited Indra no end. All day long, all he had thought about was how he would bring her to Amravati, the capital of Indraloka, so that the wealth stayed with him.

As he turned to the right, he knew she was near. Lakshmi's fragrance and radiance were hard to miss, and could be experienced way before she could be seen.

'She won't come willingly, maybe I should scare her with my mighty sword,' thought Indra, drawing his sword.

Lakshmi saw Indra, sitting atop Airavata, turn the corner. The goddess's aura rivalled the brilliance of a thousand suns. Her intense light rendered Indra blind, he lost his balance and fell off Airavata. The sword fell from his hand.

Lakshmi was amused.

'Indra, did you think you would scare me?' Lakshmi laughed. 'I have some news for you. I had decided that the first creature I see on my walk today will be my vaahana. From now on, you will be my vaahana.' With a touch of her hand, Lakshmi transformed the thousand-eyed Indra into a thousand-feathered owl, uluka. The transformation was both majestic and humbling.

The gods, witnessing this extraordinary event, gathered around and pleaded with Lakshmi. 'Oh, gracious goddess, if our king becomes a bird, who will rule over us?' they asked, their voices filled with concern.

Lakshmi, ever wise and compassionate, responded, 'Fear not, my divine companions. During the day, Indra will continue to rule the heavens as before. But at night, he will serve as my vaahana.'

So it was that Indra ruled the heavens with wisdom and justice during the day; but when night fell, he dutifully carried Lakshmi through the cosmic realms.

Did you know?

It is said that all the food at the Jagannatha ('Jagannatha' is another name for Vishnu in his Krishna avatar) temple in Puri, Odisha, is cooked by goddess Lakshmi herself, or under her supervision. It is also said that, the food does not release its aroma until it is offered to the deity.

 Sita Mai Temple in Karnal, Haryana; Sita Kund in Munger, Bihar; Seetha Eliya Seethai Amman Thirukkovil (also known as Ashok Vatika Sita Temple) in, Nuwara Eliya, Sri Lanka

 Sitanavami

SITA

DAUGHTER OF THE EARTH

Sita is the wife of Rama (Vishnu's avatar) and a central figure in the epic Ramayana. She is known for her grace, kindness, strength and wisdom. She is an incarnation of Lakshmi.

Sita was found in a furrow as a baby by King Janaka of Mithila. He adopted her and raised her as his own. She grew up to become a sensible, sensitive, strong, determined and resilient woman. She married Rama after the swayamvara organised by her father.

Sita and Rama are the perfect couple, symbolising love and devotion. In the north, they are called 'Siyarama', inseparable from each other, like light from the sun.

Sita chose to accompany Rama when he was exiled to the forest for fourteen years. She was as comfortable in the forest as she was in the palace and brought happiness wherever she went. She was abducted by Ravana, the king of Lanka, but remained strong and faithful to Rama.

> When you are courageous and resilient and stand up for what is right, you are Sita.

Did you know?

It is believed that Sita was born in either Janakpur in present-day Nepal or in Sitamarhi in Bihar.

A BLADE OF GRASS

Ravana, the ten-headed demon king, had kidnapped Sita while Rama and Lakshmana were away and brought her to Lanka. Lanka had all the wealth that one could imagine. It glittered with gold. It gleamed with riches. It teemed with lush green trees and beautiful flowers. It was surrounded by shimmering sand and the vast deep blue sea.

But what good is beauty if it brings no joy? Sita saw beauty all around, but it did not touch her.

'This is where you will stay, Sita, till you agree to marry me and become my queen,' thundered Ravana as he brought her to Ashoka Vatika, the beautiful garden of Ashoka trees.

'Get her whatever she needs, and I will give you whatever you want,' he said to the women surrounding him, twirling his moustache. 'She won't be here very long. She will soon be in my palace, my new queen!'

Sita looked him in the eye, and shaking with rage, said, 'Not even in your dreams will you see me near you. You are such a coward, you abducted me like a thief. My Rama will come not just to get me but to fight you and end your tyranny.'

The women standing around Sita could not imagine what they heard. A woman talking like that to Ravana! Did she not know his strength?

Ravana was stunned into silence at Sita's words. No woman had ever spoken to him like that.

'We will see when your Rama comes, if he comes at all!' he said and left.

She is different, murmured the women. They brought her all that they thought she would want or need. But Sita was not interested. She worried about the worries Rama and Lakshmana would have for her. How were they? How would they find her? When would they find her?

Ravana tried to entice Sita with jewels and perfumes and anything that one could ever want, but it did not work. He tried to please her by singing songs to her, but that did not work. He tried to scare her, too. That didn't work either. Nothing worked.

Sita sat under an Ashoka tree. Unshaken by the threats of Ravana. Her faith calmed her and brought her patience. She picked a blade of grass and placed it on her right. 'This is Rama,' she said.

Whenever Ravana came to her, she would hold up the blade of grass. Looking fiercely and directly into his eyes, she would say, 'I dare you come closer!'

Ravana could do nothing but retreat.

Sita's love for Rama and her sincerity scared him.

Radhaashtami

Radha Madan Mohan temple and Radha Raman temple in Vrindavan, Uttar Pradesh; Radha Rani temple in Barsana, Uttar Pradesh

RADHA
KRISHNA'S LOVER

Radha is the closest friend and lover of Krishna. She is pure with a powerful love, devotion, and spiritual longing. Her love has no boundaries. She is a form of Lakshmi.

Born in the village of Barsana near Vrindavan in Uttar Pradesh to Kirtida and Vrishabhanu, Radha is a kind, playful, happy and an adventurous girl. She is a gopi, a milkmaid, and has many other gopi friends.

A beautiful young girl and then woman, she is a bit older to Krishna. They grew up together and their friendship is special because it is selfless. They are playful, happy and completely devoted to each other to the extent that if Radha gets hurt, Krishna feels the pain. They are called Radhakrishna, inseparable and one.

Krishna wanders around Vrindavan playfully doing mischief with the gopis. When he plays the flute, Radha and all other gopis dance with such joy that they forget everything.

On beautiful nights, Krishna plays his flute in the forest. Hearing his melodious performance, the gopis sneak out of their homes and run towards him. They form a circle around him and dance around him. They all love Krishna so much that each gopi thinks Krishna is dancing with her, but Krishna, standing in the centre, dances with Radha. They dance all night not realising how much time has passed. The dance is called the 'raas leela' and reflects pure, eternal love.

Radha is the strength of Krishna. Krishna enchants the world and Radha enchants Krishna.

THE STORY OF COLOUR

Young Krishna was grumpy today. He stomped to his mother, Yashoda.

'Why am I the colour I am? I want to be like Radha. She is so pretty!'

'Your colour is beautiful, Krishna. Have you seen anyone else like yourself? My Krishna is special!' Yashoda said.

'I don't want to be special. It's not fair. I don't want to be different. I want to be like Radha!' Krishna was not appeased.

'I have an idea! You can colour Radha any colour you want, and not just Radha, anyone!' said Yashoda. 'She can be of any colour but she will remain your dear friend Radha. Colour doesn't change a person, Krishna. I have some colours in the basket behind the door, take whichever you like for Radha,' she said smiling.

Krishna's face lit up; mischief was back on his mind! He dashed to the basket, picked up a few colours and hid them, then ran out of the house. He found Radha by the river, playing with other gopis. He tiptoed behind her with fists full of colour and, when she least expected, playfully smeared her face with it.

Radha and the gopis were caught unaware but burst out laughing and chased him with their water pots, eventually drenching him!

Since then, the joyous festival of Holi is celebrated with colour, water, music and a playful spirit.

> In the towns of Barsana and Nandgaon in Uttar Pradesh, the festival of Holi begins with the ritual of Lathmar Holi, where women playfully chase men with sticks. This ritual recreates the playful teasing between Krishna and Radha.

Did you know?

Holi is celebrated for 40 days in the Braj region where Radha and Krishna were born. In Vrindavan, phoolon-wali Holi is played, where people celebrate by tossing fresh flower petals at one another.

HINDU GODS AND GODDESSES

 Annapoorna Devi mandir in Varanasi in Uttar Pradesh; Annapoorneshwari temple in Cherukunnu, Kerala; Annapoorneshwari temple in Horanadu, Karnataka

 Gowri Habba, Annapoorna Jayanti

PARVATI
GODDESS OF NOURISHMENT AND FERTILITY

Parvati is the goddess of nourishment and fertility. She is the shakti of Shiva. Theirs is an eternal love story. She has had several lives and been the partner of Shiva in each. Together they represent the perfect balance of feminine and masculine energies.

Parvati is all about strength, devotion and compassion. She has a gentle demeanour but embodies formidable powers. Parvati is the nurturing, loving aspect of Shakti. She has two arms, wears all colours of clothes and is a family woman. She is the force that makes Shiva participate in the world. She is the mother of Ganesha and Kartikeya.

Parvati and Shiva are quite opposite in nature. Parvati is lively and vivacious; she expresses love, anger and all other emotions; she likes exploring, going to different places and meeting people. Shiva is quiet and meditative; not concerned about what he wears, how he looks; not even what there is for dinner. He is comfortable as and where he is. She, the goddess of nourishment, and he, the god of destruction, make the ideal couple.

> When you nurture an idea, a thought or even a plant and reflect strength, devotion and compassion, you are Parvati.
>
> Parvati is Durga in rage and Kali in restructuring.

PURUSH/ SHAKTI

PARVATI'S POT OF RICE

Parvati and Shiva often enjoyed a game of dice at Mount Kailasa. One day, they were so drawn into the game that they began betting. Shiva put his trident at stake and Parvati her jewellery. Parvati lost the first game but won all those that followed. Shiva first lost his trident and then his snake. He was so upset at losing that he decided to go to Darukavana, the deodar forest, to clear his mind, where he met Vishnu. Shiva told him all about the game and how he lost his trident and even his snake!

Vishnu listened with patience and calmed him down. 'Go and play the game with Parvati again,' he suggested. 'You will win back everything.'

Shiva returned and said he wanted to play again. Parvati agreed. This time, Shiva won one game after another! What had changed, Parvati wondered? When Shiva's winning spree continued, she became suspicious. 'What are you up to?' she asked. 'There is more to these wins.'

'Are you cheating? I don't play with cheats,' she fumed.

An argument followed. It became so big and so loud that Vishnu appeared.

'The truth is that the dice moved the way I wanted it to,' he said to Parvati. 'Shiva thought he was playing the game, and he was right because he was. But it was I who moved the dice according to my wish. You and Shiva were under the illusion that you were playing the game, but I was making things happen,' Vishnu explained.

'Everything is maya, an illusion,' said Shiva. 'The world is an illusion. Nature is an illusion, even food is maya, an illusion,' he continued.

'Food is maya? Is that what you think?' fumed Parvati.

If food was an illusion, all the nurturing of life that she did lovingly, diligently, sincerely was an illusion. Then she, too, was an illusion.

'If I am an illusion, I am not needed,' said Parvati and disappeared from the world.

In that instant everything stopped.

There was no movement. Nature came to a standstill. Seasons did not change. It did not rain, crops withered, fruits and vegetables shrivelled. People suffered droughts and famine. Lands became barren.

Shiva realised that not every material thing was maya or illusion, and thus not needed. He understood that he was wrong to dismiss food and the nurturing of all life as maya. He recognised that food was necessary for sustenance of nature. He knew that without his shakti, Parvati, he was incomplete.

However, Parvati could not bear to see the widespread suffering of people and appeared in Kashi to distribute food.

People from near and far came to be blessed by the food she prepared and distributed.

Word reached Shiva that a goddess had appeared in Kashi distributing rice from a golden vessel. She was beautiful and kind. No matter how many ladles of food she served, the vessel overflowed with rice. They called her Annapoorna Devi, the goddess of abundance and generosity.

In his heart Shiva knew it was Parvati who had taken the form of Annapoorna Devi. He went to Kashi and stood waiting with his begging bowl with everyone else. Parvati filled his bowl. They both smiled at each other, realising that though they are different in what they do, they complete each other because of their differences.

> It is believed that when food is prepared with love and devotion, Annapoorna blesses it, and when someone wastes food, she takes note of it.
>
> At the Annapoorneshwari temple at Cherukunnu, Kerala, a packet of food is left tied to a branch of a tree every night after everyone has been fed. This is because it is said that Annapoorna believes that even a thief prowling about at night should not go hungry.

Did you know?

Parvati is believed to have served food to people as Annapoorna at the Annapoorna Devi Mandir in Varanasi. Food is distributed free of charge at this temple even today.

DURGA
GODDESS OF COURAGE AND PROTECTION

PURUSH/ SHAKTI

Durga is the most powerful warrior and the destroyer of sin and ignorance.

She is radiant, smiling, has big sharp eyes and is dressed in a red sari. She has long black hair and wears a crown. She has eight arms. In them she holds Shiva's trishula (trident); Vishnu's discus, the Sudarshana Chakra; Varuna's shankha (conch); Vayu's dhanushbana (bow and arrow); Yama's khadga (sword) and khetaka (shield); Kubera's gada (mace); Vishwakarma's parashu (axe) and a lotus flower. Her vaahana is a lion.

Durga embodies all the roles traditionally performed by different gods, and she does so in domains typically dominated by male deities.

> You are Durga when you fight for what is right, stand up against bullies and for those in need. Like Durga, you possess strength, courage and the ability to stand up against injustice.

 Singha

 Durga Puja, Navaratri

 Trishula, Sudarshana Chakra, dhanush-bana, khadga, khetaka, gada, parashu

 Vaishno Devi in Jammu and Kashmir; Danteshwari temple in Dantewada, Chhattisgarh

MAHISHASURAMARDINI

Mahishasura was strong and aggressive. His mother was a buffalo and father an asura. People near and far had heard stories of his strength and aggression. They had also heard stories of how evil he was. That's why everyone everywhere was shocked when news went around that he had decided to go in deep prayer to Brahma.

Mahishasura gave up food. Then he gave up water. He stood on one leg under a tree and remained like that for years praying to Brahma. His hair touched the grass and creepers grew over them, but he remained in prayer. Steadfast. Years passed by, but Mahishasura did not even move, sway, let alone put his other leg down. He stood firmly on one leg and stayed in prayer, year after year.

Brahma was pleased with his devotion and appeared before him.

'Ask what you wish for, and I will grant it,' said Brahma.

Mahishasura had imagined this scene several times over in his mind. He had waited all these years to ask for a boon.

'I would like to become immortal and live forever,' Mahishasura said without wasting a minute.

'That is not possible. All those who are born must die and be reborn again. That is the nature of life, the universal law,' said Brahma. 'Ask for anything else.'

Mahishasura thought about what he could ask for that would make his end difficult. 'In that case, grant me a boon that I cannot be killed by a man or a god. If I must die, it must be at the hands of a woman.'

'Tathaastu, so be it,' said Brahma and disappeared.

Smug at being granted the boon, Mahishasura laughed to himself, 'A woman killing me! Ha! That is as good as being immortal!'

Filled with arrogance like never before, Mahishasura put all his evil plans of destruction into action. He attacked humans on earth, defeated them and destroyed everything around them. Next on his plan was to fight the gods.

He led his army of asuras and attacked Amravati, the capital of Indraloka. Indra did his best to fight Mahishasura but lost. Mahishasura had become invincible. No man or god could defeat him.

Indra rushed to Brahma, Vishnu and Mahesha (which is another name for Shiva) for help. 'Mahishasura destroyed earth and Amravati, I am too afraid to even imagine what he will do next.'

Brahma recalled the boon he had given Mahishasura. No man or god could kill him. He would die at the hands of a woman. But where was such a woman? There wasn't. So, Brahma, Vishnu and Mahesha decided to create a woman who would not just be a formidable match to the strength of Mahishasura but would be much stronger and more powerful.

The three gods concentrated on their energies. A mass of pure energy so bright that it dimmed even the light of Surya appeared in the sky. From this they created Durga, who would be as formidable as an unassailable fortress.

Shiva created her face, Vishnu her arms and Brahma her legs. Varuna gave her a red sari and a diamond necklace. Vishwakarma, the celestial designer and architect made earrings, bangles, anklets and other jewellery for her. Vishnu gave her his Sudarshana Chakra, Shiva his trishula and Brahma his lotus and kamandala, his water pot of holy water and wisdom. Other gods gave her different things too. She got a lion as a mount, and she set out to find Mahishasura.

Mountains shook and waves soared as she reached closer to him. Word reached Mahishasura that a woman was on her way and his end was near. Mahishasura laughed so hard that he fell off his chair. 'A woman thinks she can kill me? She has no idea. A few of my men will manage whatever "threat" she is!'

One by one, all the men that Mahishasura sent met their end at the hands of Durga. When there were no men left, Mahishasura went himself. The minute he faced her, he knew she was as formidable as a fortress, true to her name Durga. He took the form of a lion and even an elephant to attack her, but she stood firm. They battled each other for eight days and eight nights without letting up.

On the ninth day, Mahishasura took the form of a buffalo to attack Durga and mow her down. But Durga used Vishnu's Sudarshana Chakra and Mahishasura met his end.

Life and order were restored, and peace returned to all the worlds. To celebrate this victory over evil, one that took nine days coming, Hindus celebrate the festival of Navaratri, which literally means nine nights, and Durga Puja. On the ninth day of the Navaratris, Durga is called Mahishasuramardini, the one who killed Mahishasura.

 Khadga, trishula

 Kali Puja, Navaratri

 Dakshineswar Kali mandir in Kolkata, West Bengal; Sree Badhrakali Dewaswom Temple in Kollemcode village, Kanyakurai, Tamil Nadu

KALI
GODDESS OF TANSFORMATION

Kali is the transformative force of Shakti that destroys and makes recreation possible.

She is dark complexioned, fierce looking, powerful and completely in control. She has big bloodshot eyes and her tongue sticks out her mouth. She wears a garland of skulls, and the only garment she wears is a garland made of dead men's hands. She has long, black untied hair and four arms. In them she holds a khadga (sword), trishula (trident), a bowl and the head of the demon she has killed.

Kali is fiercely protective of her devotees and kills egos.

> You are Kali when you are fearless, overcome obstacles, embrace change and bring positive transformation around you.

KALI AND HER RED TONGUE

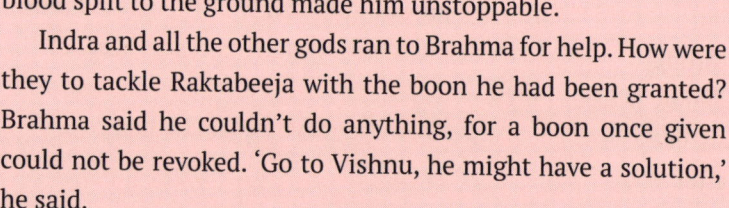

Raktabeeja won a boon from Brahma that if a drop of his rakta (blood) fell on the ground, it would turn into a beeja (seed) and sprout a duplicate of himself. Raktabeeja went about on a rampage. His ability to produce even more trouble when a drop of his blood spilt to the ground made him unstoppable.

Indra and all the other gods ran to Brahma for help. How were they to tackle Raktabeeja with the boon he had been granted? Brahma said he couldn't do anything, for a boon once given could not be revoked. 'Go to Vishnu, he might have a solution,' he said.

'I don't know how we can get over this problem. Go to Shiva, he might have an idea,' said Vishnu.

'I don't know how we can stop Raktabeeja. That boon has made it impossible,' said Shiva. 'Let me ask Shakti.'

Shakti took the form of the fierce and formidable Kali. She prepared herself for the battle, a garland of skulls around her neck and a girdle of dead men's hands at her waist. Her tongue stuck out, eager to lap up every single drop of blood before it would spill to the ground.

Seething with anger at the devastation Raktabeeja had caused her devotees, the goddess charged towards him to put an end to his evil intentions and deeds.

Kali faced Raktabeeja, piercing him with the gaze of her red eyes. With a swift movement of her khadga, the demon's head was in her hand. She drained every drop of his blood; her tongue turned blood red.

GANGA
RIVER GODDESS

The majestic river goddess is the goddess of purification and forgiveness. She travels through all the three worlds, heaven, earth and atmosphere.

She is beautiful, fair-skinned, eternally pure, graceful and melodious. She wears a white crown and is usually dressed in white. She moves sometimes like a shy girl, sometimes like a nurturing mother and sometimes like a graceful athlete leaping through the mountains.

She is the daughter of Himalaya and Menaka, and the elder sister of Parvati. Bhagirath brought Ganga from heaven to earth after centuries of prayer for his ancestors' salvation. As she touched the earth she also blessed all of humanity, spreading auspiciousness. She holds a water lily and a pot of water in her hands. She is kind and sympathetic towards all. Her vaahana is a makara, whose body is like that of a ghariyal and tail like that of a fish.

Ganga moves through mountains, plains and cities, bringing life to all in her path. She provides nourishment, frees us from ignorance and brings clarity to our thoughts. Just a few drops of the Ganga are believed to purify, cleans and heal all that they are sprinkled on.

> In the Bhagavad Gita (10.31), Krishna says that of the rivers he is Ganga.

When the Ganga meets the Bay of Bengal, its mouth forms the largest river delta of the world. It is called the Ganges River Delta.

 Makara

 Gangotri in Uttarakhand; the banks of the Ganga in places such as Haridwar, Prayagraj and Varanasi

 Kumbh Mela, Ganga Dussehra

GANGA AND HER MANY NAMES

Sage Bhagirath realised that the only way the souls of his ancestors could attain peace was by having their ashes washed by the water of the holy river Ganga. Though his ancestors had also prayed for Ganga to descend to earth, they had been unsuccessful. But Bhagirath was determined; he sat in penance and prayed to Ganga for centuries.

Pleased by his sincerity to his ancestors the goddess agreed to come to earth as a river, but there was a problem. Ganga with her energy and nature was too big a force for earth. She flowed at such great speed that the entire planet could be washed away. Bhagirath now needed the help of Shiva as only he had the power to receive and channelise her rambunctious but pure, healing waters.

Bhagirath sat deep in prayer to Shiva. Pleased with Bhagirath's devotion, Shiva smiled and agreed to grant his wish. Just as Ganga came rushing and singing, he took her in his matted hair, absorbing the impact of her force and power. Eternally grateful, Bhagirath requested Shiva to release Ganga from his locks so that she could reach the ashram where the ashes of his ancestors had waited for generations and centuries to be purified.

'Lead the way and blow the shankha, the conch to clear a path,' said Shiva as he gently squeezed a lock of his hair to release Ganga. Ganga followed Bhagirath curious and excited and bringing new life to the lands in her path.

They reached the ashram of Rishi Jahnu, where a yagna was underway. The sounds of hundreds of humans chanting mantras on earth was new to her. Curiosity got the better of her. She went

ahead to check it out and as she did, the rushing river swept everything away. The entire ashram was flooded, the sacrificial fire extinguished and everything began to float!

Rishi Jahnu lost his temper and took Ganga's curiosity for arrogance, as a show of power. He drank the entire river in the next instant.

Bhagirath prayed again, this time to Rishi Jahnu requesting him to release Ganga. Rishi Jahnu finally released Ganga through his ear. That is why Ganga is also called Jahnvi.

Finally, Bhagirath was able to bring Ganga to where the ashes of his ancestors lay. Ganga brought them peace. Bhagirath's efforts in bringing Ganga from heaven brought salvation to his ancestors and turned all the lands Ganga touched fertile. That is why Ganga is also called Bhagirathi.

> Bhagirath's efforts are iconic. A task extremely difficult to achieve is referred to as 'Bhagirath prayaas' in Hindi.

Did you know?

The Kumbh Mela is the largest congregation of pilgrims on earth. Millions of people attend this festival seeking liberation from the cycle of birth and death by taking a dip in a sacred river. The festival is held by turns at Prayagraj (where the Ganga, Yamuna and Saraswati are said to meet) and Haridwar (Ganga), Nasik (Godavari) and Ujjain (Shipra) every four years. The Kumbh Mela is based on a distinct set of astrological positions of the Sun, Moon and Jupiter. The holiest time occurs at the exact moment when these positions are fully occupied.

The rock on which Bhagirath sat for penance is called Bhagirath Shila and is at Gangotri. It is believed that this is where Ganga first touched earth.

 Kurma

 Yamunotri temple, Uttarakhand

 Yamuna Chhat

YAMUNA
RIVER GODDESS

Yamuna represents purification, salvation, love and compassion. She is beautiful and dark skinned, and has a beautiful smile. Her teeth shine like stars and her arms are gracefully swaying waves. She holds a pot in one hand. This river goddess is the daughter of Agni and Sanjana (also known as Sharanya), and the twin sister of Yama.

She originates from the mountain Kalinda and so is also called Kalindi. Her waters purify, cleansing the mind of sins. Her vaahana is Kurma, a tortoise.

She is a goddess of infinite love and compassion. She and Krishna have been companions since his birth. She kept him company in both Mathura and Vrindavan, while he played his flute to her. Yamuna's love for Krishna runs deep; her skin is also dark like Krishna's.

Ganga and Yamuna are usually seen on either side of temple gates. Passing through these is said to be purifying.

> Legend has it that Yamuna wished that her devotees could be more comfortable when they came to visit her at the Yamunotri glacier. When she spoke with Surya, her father, he gifted her a single ray that touches the Divya Shila (divine stone). Boiling water emerges from the Divya Shila and devotees cook rice and potatoes in little muslin parcels before visiting the Yamunotri temple!

YAMUNA AND YAMA

Yamuna and Yama squabbled like all siblings. They were also, like all siblings, each other's strongest supporters. Some days they fought fiercely, endlessly, and on others they were inseparable, boisterous best friends.

Once Yama became the guide of the dead, his work kept him extremely busy. Yamuna and Yama were able to spend less and less time together. Yamuna wished for him to visit her, but his round-the-clock schedule made it difficult. They kept in touch, but it wasn't the same as being together.

One day Yama said, 'Enough of non-stop work! I will meet my sister today, come what may.' The day was kartika shukla dwitiya, the second day of the bright fortnight of the month of Kartik. (Usually, this falls in the months of October and November in the Gregorian calendar.) There was a spring in his step, a smile on his face and his heart brimmed with love for his sister as he left Yamaloka to meet Yamuna. Memories of all the fun they had together as they grew up made him so happy that he released some trapped souls on the way.

Yamuna was overjoyed to see him. Her face lit up, her eyes twinkled and she just couldn't stop smiling. Finally, he was here! Yamuna prepared a feast for Yama, remembering all the things that he loved. She put a tilak on his forehead that started perfectly from between his eyebrows and went up to the crown of his head. She wished him strength and wisdom, peace and success. There was nothing she wanted more in that moment.

It was a day they enjoyed equally together.

When it was time to leave, Yama asked Yamuna to ask for a boon. 'Ask for whatever you wish Yamuna, I will grant it. You are the best sister—thoughtful, caring, understanding, and you do not shy away from saying exactly what you think to me. I know you always wish the best for me.'

Yamuna did not take long. 'Promise me that you will visit me on this day every year. Promise me also that every brother who visits his sister on this day, and every sister who applies a tika on her brother's forehead and serves him food with love will not fear your presence, Yama.'

'Tathaastu, so be it!'

'Yamuna, I have another gift for you. Those brothers and sisters who hold each other's hand and take a dip in your flowing waters on this special day will not have any cause to fear me or face my wrath.'

A day that was special to Yama and Yamuna became a special day for all siblings. Since then, every year brothers and sisters celebrate Bhai Dooj, knowing that Yamuna and Yama will protect their relationship and that no matter how far they are, their love will always keep them together.

TRIDEVA /TRINITY
THE HOLY TRINITY

Together Brahma, Vishnu and Mahesha (Shiva) are known as Trideva (the three gods). They work together to create, preserve and transform the universe. They help keep everything in balance and ensure that life can continue in harmony.

BRAHMA
THE CREATOR

PURUSH/ TRIDEVA

Brahma is the creator of the universe. He created gods and then placed them in their respective worlds (e.g. Surya in the sky, Vayu in the atmosphere and Agni in our world.)

He has red skin, white hair and sports a white beard. He has four heads, and infinite knowledge. The four heads show that he is present in all four directions. He also has four arms and holds the Vedas, which he created; a mala (rosary) that symbolises time; a sruva (ladle) for pouring ghee into the sacrificial fire and a kamandala (water pot) symbolising creation. Brahma carries no weapons.

He wears white, sits on a lotus and rides a hansa (swan). The hansa can separate milk form water.

Gods often consult him when faced with problems. He is generous in giving blessings and boons, and can give boons that he later regrets.

He is one-third of the Trimurti, the holy trinity, along with Vishnu and Mahesha. His partner is Saraswati.

Like Brahma, you have the power to create and shape your own world.

Have you heard of the Brahma Muhurta? It means the creator's time. It is believed to be the best time for creating, learning and planning. It begins 1 hour and 36 minutes before sunrise and ends 48 minutes before it.

HINDU GODS AND GODDESSES

 Hansa

 Ugadi

 Jagatpita Brahma Temple in Pushkar, Rajasthan

BRAHMA'S LIE

Brahma and Vishnu quarrelled often. It was always about who is better. Brahma said he was superior because he created the world. Vishnu said that didn't make him better—it proved that he was not; god wouldn't go about trying to prove that he was god! Moreover, what good is a god if he cannot sustain the world he creates?

'I sustain the world. Therefore, I am of greater importance than you!' retorted Vishnu.

They went on and on until suddenly an agnistambha, a huge pillar of fire, appeared between them. The crackling of the agnistambha's blaze drowned all sound.

Brahma and Vishnu stilled in shock, their eyes and mouths wide open. This pillar of fire had appeared from nowhere, and it didn't seem to have a beginning or end!

Their competitive spirit kicked in, and now it was about who would find the end of the fire pillar first. Brahma took the form of a swan set off to investigate how high the fire blazed and flew up. Vishnu took the form of a boar and began digging down. For days, weeks, months and years Brahma flew up, up and up, but there was no sight of the top of the pillar. Similarly, Vishnu dug deep, then deeper and even deeper, but there was no end in sight. The agnistambha seemed to come from and go into infinity.

Exhausted beyond exhaustion the two decided to end their search. 'This pillar has no end,' Vishnu said panting. 'It has a beginning though,' Brahma said panting and lying through his teeth, 'I saw the top and the ketaki flowers on top of it too!'

Just as the words left his mouth, the Agnistambha flared wide. A figure smeared in ash strode towards the two. It was Shiva!

Furious at Brahma's deceit, he said, 'Your ego is bigger than you. You cannot be God.'

He turned to Vishnu, and his anger turned to a smile, 'You speak the truth and accept your limitations. You could become God.'

Two things happened then.

Brahma's worshippers became fewer and fewer (that is why there are hardly any Brahma temples). And the linga, a stone symbolizing the agnistambha, began to be worshipped.

The Arunachaleswarar temple in Thiruvannamalai, Tamil Nadu, is where the agnistambha is said to have appeared.

Did you know?

Did you know that the Brahmaastra is a weapon created by Brahma meant to be used only as a last resort, it can cause indescribable destruction.

 Garuda

 Sudarshana Chakra, gada

 Shankha

 Vishu, Ramnavami, Krishna Janmaashtami

 Badrinath temple in Badrinath, Uttarakhand; Sri Venkateswara Swamy Temple in Tirumala, Andhra Pradesh; Padmanabhaswamy Temple in Thiruvananthapuram, Kerala

VISHNU
THE PROTECTOR

Vishnu is the protector of the universe. He preserves and sustains the universe and upholds dharma, the path of virtue, duty and righteousness.

Vishnu is handsome; he has big, beautiful eyes and a mesmerising smile. He has bluish skin, reflecting the colour of the cosmos—of the limitless skies, oceans and rain-bearing clouds. He has four hands and in them he holds a shankha (conch), chakra (discus), gada (mace) and padma (pink lotus). He wears yellow silk, a jewelled crown, the ruby red-gem named Kaustubha and the Vaijayanti Mala, the garland of rare gems. His vaahana is Garuda, the king of birds.

Vishnu is patient, calm and peaceful. He is usually seen resting on the thousand-headed serpent king, Shesha.

He incarnates on earth in every age to destroy evil forces, protect the good and preserve dharma. Rama and Krishna are his avatars.

He is offered fruits, flowers, ghee, water, sweets, clothes and ornaments.

His partner is Lakshmi. She is the shakti that makes Vishnu complete. They live in Vaikuntha with fine luxuries.

He has ten avatars or incarnations. Nine of them have been born:

1. Matsya, the fish
2. Kurma or Kachchap, the turtle
3. Varaaha, the boar
4. Narsimha, the man-lion

5. Vaamana, the dwarf
6. Parashurama, the angry warrior
7. Rama, the perfect man
8. Krishna, the perfect player
9. Buddha, the enlightened one
10. Kalki

Many scholars see the ten avatars of Vishnu reflecting the theory of evolution. Evolution is the idea that all living things came from earlier forms of life. The differences we see now are because of changes that happened over a long time.

You are Vishnu when you protect and preserve harmony around you; embrace compassion, kindness and responsibility; and do good.

The Kaustubha, the divine red ruby that Vishnu sports, came out of Samudramanthana. It is said to be a most magnificent gem.

Named after Vishnu, who maintains balance in the universe, the Vishnu Mudra is a hand position in yoga used for alternate nostril-breathing techniques. This mudra promotes balance.

VISHNU LOCKS SHIVA OUT!

Narada, a sage, storyteller, and an avid traveller, travelled across all spheres chatting with everyone he met. He had a mischievous streak and loved getting people worked up.

He stopped by at Vaikuntha one day. As usual, Vishnu was lounging on the Sheshanaag, and Lakshmi was by his side offering him something to eat.

'Vishnu, what example are you setting for those on the planet? You laze around all day while Lakshmi takes care of you! Don't you think you should do something more meaningful, something that has a higher purpose?'

Those words got Vishnu thinking and he decided to leave for the Himalayas.

In the Himalayas, Vishnu found a place called Badrinath. It was calm and beautiful. It seemed like the ideal place to meditate and contemplate. He saw a little house there and fell in love with it. There was something about the house and the setting that attracted him. The doors were wide open, and Vishnu couldn't help himself—he couldn't resist going in.

Everything seemed perfect until he entered the house. As soon as he stepped in Vishnu realised that this was the house of Shiva and Parvati. He knew that though Shiva is kind and easy to please, he can also get angry very quickly. And when he gets angry, he can do anything.

Unwilling to face Shiva's wrath, Vishnu cooked up an idea. He transformed himself into a toddler and sat waiting there.

When Shiva and Parvati returned home, they found a bonny baby gurgling at their door. The baby looked at them and smiled. Enchanted by the baby, Parvati bent down to pick it up.

'Don't do that. Let the child be. This isn't what you think it is,' warned Shiva.

'How cold-hearted can you be to tell me to leave a child out in the cold? What will happen to it, it is snowing!' Parvati reprimanded.

'Exactly my point,' said Shiva, 'There is snow all around. This child just appears from nowhere, no adult around, no footmarks in the snow!'

'Why do you always think the opposite of what I think? I am taking this munchkin inside and getting it something to eat.'

The baby cooed and squealed, enjoyed a snack of fruits, and played peek-a-boo with Parvati. It looked at Shiva and giggled.

Soon, it was time for Shiva and Parvati to go to the hot springs. Parvati settled the baby down for a nap and in the split of a second the baby was fast asleep. What a good baby, thought Parvati!

All the way to the hot springs and back, Parvati could only talk about the baby. But when they got home, they found it locked from the inside.

'Who could have done that!' Parvati was aghast.

'Your cooing baby, Parvati. The one you played peek-a-boo with, fed fruits and even sang a lullaby to. I tried to stop you, but… You took the child inside and now that child has locked us out!'

'What should we do now?' Parvati said.

Shiva could have burnt the house down in an instant, but he decided instead to find another house.

Parvati and Shiva found a home in Kedarnath. Vishnu continued to live in Badrinath.

Did you know?

Vishnu has a thousand names and the Vishnu Sahasranaama is a Sanskrit hymn that lists the thousand names of Vishnu that Bhishma recited in the war of Kurukshetra in the Mahabharata.

	Nandi		Trishula and the bow named Pinaaka
	Damaru		Kedarnath temple in Kedarnath, Uttarakhand; Thillai Nataraja temple in Chidambaram, Tamil Nadu; Shri Kashi Vishwanath temple in Varanasi, Uttar Pradesh
	Maha Shivaratri		

SHIVA
THE DESTROYER

Shiva is the god of destruction, preparing the world for renewal. He is Mahadeva, the greatest of gods; Adi Guru, the first guru; and Adiyogi, the first yogi.

He appears grey, because his body is smeared with ash. His throat is blue—it holds the Halaahala, the poison that emerged from the churning of the ocean and threatened to destroy the world. He has three eyes; if opened, the third eye unleashes energy so powerful that it can cause destruction. He wears a jata mukuta, his long, flowing dreadlocks tied in a topknot like a crown, and it is adorned with the crescent moon and Ganga. Ganga flows through his matted hair, cleansing and purifying all she touches, while the crescent moon symbolises the cycle of time. Vasuki, the king of serpents, is coiled around his neck, and he wears a garland of skulls.

He is dressed in animal hide. He carries a trishula (trident) and plays the damaru, a two-headed drum. He is often depicted as sitting cross-legged, deep in meditation, indicating great peace and stability. He rides the bull named Nandi, who represents independence, strength, loyalty and devotion.

He lives at Mount Kailasa with his partner Shakti, also known as Parvati, Uma, Durga-Kali. They have two children, Ganesha and Kartikeya.

Shiva embodies both fierce strength and serene wisdom, and he is as quick to please as he is to anger. Tandava, his cosmic dance, symbolises the eternal rhythm of creation, preservation-destruction. In his dancing form, Shiva is called Nataraja, the king or lord of dance.

WHEN SHIVA'S BOON BECAME HIS BANE

Shiva was kind to his devotees. One of them had been praying to him for hundreds of years. Hunger, thirst, harsh winters, scorching summers—none of these could stop Bhasmasura's devotion. If there was any thought in his mind it was about Shiva. If he spoke a word, it was Shiva. If he had a dream, it was about Shiva. Shiva was touched by such devotion and thought it was time to bless Bhasmasura.

One morning as Bhasmasura sat deep in prayer, Shiva appeared. 'Ask—what do you desire?' said Shiva. Bhasmasura couldn't believe his luck! He pinched himself so hard that it left a bruise. I must be so good that Shiva actually appeared before me, Bhasmasura gloated.

Bhasmasura knew what he wanted from the day he started praying to Shiva. 'Lord, grant me this boon. Whoever's head I touch should reduce to ash in an instant.'

'Tathaastu,' said Shiva and started walking towards the mountains. Bhasmasura laughed in glee—he was going to put this hard-won boon to test right away!

He ran behind Shiva. With Shiva crumbled to ashes, Bhasmasura could become Mahadeva, the most powerful.

Shiva now understood Bhasmasura's intention. But it was too late. The boon had been granted. The god ran ahead, trishula in hand, Bhasmasura's belly laugh resounding close behind.

They ran through mountains, rivers and villages, through vast fields and thick forests. But Bhasmasura kept up the pursuit, his greed and ambition giving him the strength to keep up with Shiva.

High up in Vaikuntha, Vishnu had watched the entire scene unfold. He had to do something. He transformed into a young, beautiful dancer and appeared in front of Bhasmasura dancing gracefully to gentle music.

Bhasmasura was smitten the instant he saw her and stood transfixed. 'Who are you? I have never ever seen a dancer as graceful as you!'

She smiled secretively and said, 'You may call me Mohini.'

'Mohini,' Bhasmasura repeated as if under a spell. 'They named you well. You are indeed very attractive. Will you marry me?'

She shook her head. 'I will only marry a dancer.'

'If you can teach me, I will learn.'

'Let's see. If you can follow my dance, doing it exactly as I do, I will consider.'

Mohini drew a half circle with her leg, then shifting her stance, moved her arms upward and put her palms together like a flower. She looked at Bhasmasura challengingly.

Bhasmasura followed every movement of her hands and feet, and even managed to mirror her facial expressions. He seemed to be enjoying it. What a great dancer I am, he thought as he moved with the music. How much talent can there be in one man, Bhasmasura gloated.

With a gentle sway of her hand, Mohini placed her right hand on her head and smiled. Bhasmasura swayed his right hand gently and placed it on his head.

Before he realised his folly, Bhasmasura was reduced to ashes! Mohini turned back into Vishnu and looked at Shiva with his characteristic smile. Shiva smiled, too. The protector had protected the good and destroyed evil.

Did you know?

There are two kinds of classical dances in India. Tandava, considered vigorous and masculine, was created by Shiva, while Lasya, with its gentle, soft and feminine movements, comes from Parvati. Bharatanatyam, Kathak, Odissi and Manipuri among other classical dance forms of India incorporate both Tandava and Lasya.

KAMADEVA
GOD OF LOVE AND DESIRE

Love is a powerful force that binds the universe. It is embodied by Kamadeva, the god of love and desire. He ignites passion and affection among gods and humans alike, promoting harmony and creation. Kamadeva shoots flower-tipped arrows at people that kindle desire, wishes, infatuation and beauty in them.

He is a handsome young man, green in colour. He wears jewellery made of flowers and seated on a shuka, a green parrot. His bow is made of sugarcane, a line of bees serve as its bowstring. A quiver of arrows hangs on his back. He carries five arrows, each with a different flower at its tip—aravinda (white lotus), ashoka (flowers of the ashoka tree), choota (mango tree flowers), navamallika (jasmine) and neelotpala (blue lotus).

When Kamadeva's arrows touch your
- ♥ Heart, it makes you feel super excited and full of joyful energy.
- ♥ Lips, you can't help but shout out with happiness.
- ♥ Head, it makes you go a bit crazy with love, filling your mind with wild thoughts.
- ♥ Eyes, it makes you see everything in a magical way, like you're in a dream.
- ♥ Anywhere else, it makes you feel full of love!

Kamadeva travels the three worlds with Rati, his beautiful wife. Rati is the goddess of passion and physical attraction. Kamadeva is the most handsome young man and Rati is the prettiest young woman. Kamadeva and Rati travel together and are accompanied by a gentle breeze, cuckoos and their good friend Vasant, the spring season.

	Kamavilas / Kaman Pandigai/ Kama-Dahanam, Holi, Poorotsavam		Madan Kamdev temple in Baihata Chariali, Assam
	Madhuyasti dhanusha		Shuka

KAMADEVA ANGERS SHIVA

Shiva was devastated by the death of his wife, Sati. He lost interest in his work and went into deep meditation.

Without him, there was chaos in the world. The imbalance worried the gods. Something had to be done. The gods held a meeting. Of particular urgency was the matter of Tarakasura, the demon king who was becoming a nuisance. He could only be killed by the son of Shiva and Parvati, a reincarnation of Sati. But how was that to happen if Shiva continued to sit in meditation with his eyes closed? He needed to see Parvati, meet and marry her to have children! The gods decided that Kamadeva would shoot at Shiva with one of his arrows.

Kamadeva and Rati went to Mount Kailasa. Unaware of all this, Shiva continued his meditation. Then, Kamadeva and Rati noticed Parvati and her friends coming towards Shiva.

This is a good time, thought Kamadeva. He hid behind a tree, nocked an arrow to his bow, and aiming at Shiva, released it.

As soon as the arrow touched him, Shiva opened his eyes. His heart was immediately filled with passion at the sight of Parvati.

Shiva felt this sudden emotion, and he knew immediately that this could only be the work of Kamadeva. Furious about this, Shiva opened his third eye and looked at Kamadeva. In a fraction of a second, Kamadeva was reduced to ashes.

'Why did you do that?' an upset, heartbroken, wailing Rati asked Shiva, 'Kamadeva did what the gods wanted him to do to save the world. They said this was the only way you would come out of meditation and go back to your work—work that you have been ignoring for so long. What kind of justice is this?'

Parvati was also upset, and the gods pleaded too, but Shiva said, 'What is done is done and cannot be undone.'

With Kamadeva gone, there was no love left in the world. There was no joy, there was nothing to look forward to.

Rati prayed and meditated for forty days. Shiva felt compassion and brought the god of love back to life in a form that had no body. Ever since that day, love has been a special feeling that everyone can experience.

Shiva and Parvati went on to have a son, Kartikeya, who put an end to the evil ways of Tarakasura.

Did you know?

Kamadeva is worshipped during weddings so that he blesses the couple with love, happiness and children.

KARTIKEYA
GOD OF WAR AND VICTORY

Kartikeya is the god of war and victory. He is the commander-in-chief of the divine army and fights against demons to protect the universe from evil.

He is golden in colour, reflecting the colour of valour. He has six faces and twelve powerful arms. He is the son of Shiva and Parvati and the brother of Ganesha. He rides on a peacock, which represents beauty, grace, and watchfulness.

He carries a vela, a spear, given to him by Parvati. Kartikeya embodies bravery, leadership and triumph as well as discipline, intelligence and strategic thinking.

The god of war destroys enemies around you and inside you. He protects and inspires leaders and seekers of knowledge to reach their full potential.

He is also known as Murugan, Shanmukha, Skanda, Subramanya and Swaminatha. In temples in south India, you will find his idol facing the north, where his parents live.

> Kartikeya encourages you to find strength and courage to overcome fears and obstacles. He motivates you to be determined, to embrace leadership and bravery.

 Mayura

 Skanda Shashthi, Thaipusam

 Vela (spear)

 Kartikeya temple in Pehowa, Haryana; Dhandayuthapani Swamy temple in Palani, Tamil Nadu; NeendoorSubrahmanya Swami temple in Neendoor, Kerala

WHEN LITTLE KARTIKEYA BECAME HIS FATHER'S GURU

Brahma could be a good guru to little Kartikeya, thought Shiva and Parvati. Kartikeya was a disciplined boy and Brahma could nurture the love of learning in him. They decided to send Kartikeya to him.

Kartikeya was excited. He had so many questions, and now he officially had a teacher who would answer them. Kartikeya was armed with his first question even before he reached Brahma. As soon as he got off his vaahana, a peacock, he greeted Brahma and asked, 'Can you please tell me the meaning of Om?'

Brahma was taken aback. This was not what he was expecting! He thought it was too big a question for little Kartikeya. Moreover, he was not sure of the answer himself!

'You can't jump the gun, little fellow. You need to begin by learning the alphabets first!' Brahma said trying to wriggle out of the big question.

But Brahma could not distract Kartikeya from that question, no matter how hard he tried. Kartikeya got more and more annoyed because Brahma, the god who created the entire universe, would not answer his first and only question.

'You don't know the answer, that is why you are talking about everything else except what I want to know. I am going back home,' said Kartikeya and hopped on to his peacock and started back for home.

'Your son is beyond me, Shiva. I tried my best, but it didn't work. Only you can manage him,' said Brahma to Shiva.

Shiva was waiting outside when Kartikeya reached home. 'Brahma created the universe and the Vedas, and you think he is not a good enough teacher for you?'

'He may have created the universe but he doesn't have answers and does not even try to find answers. How can he be a good teacher if he does not believe in learning all the time?' huffed Kartikeya.

He looked up at Shiva, 'Can you tell me the meaning of Om?' Shiva smiled. 'Even I don't know what it means, Kartikeya.'

'I can explain it to you.'

'Please tell me Kartikeya. I want to know what Om means,' said Shiva.

'How can I explain it to you like this? If you want to learn something you must give the guru a higher position to sit, and you need to be seated lower than me!' Kartikeya was getting annoyed again.

Shiva lifted little Kartikeya and seated him on his shoulder. Now seated higher than Shiva, Kartikeya happily whispered into his father's ear, 'Om contains the entire creation. Brahma, Vishnu and Mahesha are all a part of it. "Om" means unbreakable, unshakeable love. "Om" means everything is love.'

Parvati was overjoyed at the depth of Kartikeya's knowledge. 'You have become a guru to my swami, my husband!' she exclaimed.

Since then, Kartikeya is also addressed as Swaminatha.

SAMANVAYA
SYMPHONY

Samanvaya, the symphony between seeming opposites—human and nature, sustenance and destruction, female and male, human and animal, Deva and Daanava, and Visha and Amrita—forms the foundation of Hindu philosophy.

HANUMAN (NARA + VAANAR)
GANESH (NARA + GAJA)
NARASIMHA (NARA + SIMHA)

HARIHARA (VISHNU + SHIVA)
ARDHANAREESHVARA (NAARI + NARA)
SAMUDRAMANTHAN (DEVA + DAANAVA, VISHA+AMRIT)

 Gada

 Hanuman Jayanti

 Sankat Mochan Hanuman mandir in Varanasi, Uttar Pradesh; Jakhu mandir in Shimla, Himachal Pradesh

HANUMAN
THE DEVOTED GOD
NARA + VAANARA

Hanuman is a god with the perfect blend of bala (strength), buddhi (intelligence) and vidya (wisdom).

This humongous god is a tawny muscular vaanar with a long tail. He is as strong and powerful as a vajra; as indestructible as a diamond and as unstoppable as a thunderbolt. He carries a gada (mace) in his hand and devotion to Rama in his heart. All planets listen to him. He appears orange because he has poured sindoor (vermilion) all over his body after Sita told him that she applied it in her hair parting for the long and healthy life of Rama.

He is curious (he is a vaanar!), and he does not want power or wealth, only knowledge. He is a scientific scholar, musician, grammarian and poet. He also plays the veena. Although he is very accomplished, he is modest and not arrogant about his knowledge or talents.

Hanuman can move at the speed of wind—after all, he is the son of Vayu! He is so strong that he can lift huge mountains, so agile that he can leap across the seas and soar across vast distances, so learned that he can recite all the Vedas, and

It is said that Hanuman introduced the practice of surya namaskar in gratitude to Surya for being his guru.

HINDU GODS AND GODDESSES

so powerful that he can increase or decrease his size at will, becoming as huge as a mountain or as tiny as an ant.

Hanuman helps Rama, the seventh avatar of Vishnu, to find his wife Sita, who was abducted by Ravana, the king of Lanka.

Hanuman is all about strength and humility. His devotion fuels his might. He teaches loyalty and shows the power of real love. He is generous and has no insecurity. Tuesday and Saturday are considered good days to pray to him.

> When you give something your absolute best because you believe in it completely, when you are in the flow of a task, when you stand by someone in need, when pride does not shadow your effort, and when you seek knowledge, you are Hanuman.

Hanuman is immortal, so could meet you anywhere and anytime! Stay on the lookout!

> Most wrestlers in India associate closely with Hanuman and seek his blessings for strength and power. That is why akharas or wrestling arenas have a photo of Hanuman.

Hanumanasana in yoga derives its name from the giant leap made by Hanuman to Lanka.

ONCE A FRUIT, NOW A GURU

Little Hanuman was extremely curious. It was in his nature but Hanuman was extra curious. Why, what, when, where and how were his favourite questions, and he never tired of asking them. He had so many questions that his mother Anjana and father Kesari thought it was time to find a guru who had the answers and could guide Hanuman.

Surya seemed like an ideal choice. He is the seer of the entire universe. He removes darkness to bring light and knowledge, he knows everything because he sees everything as he travels all around.

Though he was the perfect teacher for Hanuman, the big question was, would Surya agree?

As a toddler, Hanuman had mistaken the rising sun for a fruit and had leapt up to eat it! Cheeky little Hanuman was also known to tease sages meditating in the forest by tugging at their beard, rearranging their articles of worship or spilling their holy water!

When the parents requested Surya to be Hanuman's guru, Surya said it would not be possible since he was traveling all the time. He said, 'I am in my chariot all the time going from one place to the other. I cannot stop. How can I teach?'

Hanuman had been inspired by Surya since the first time he had seen him up close as a toddler. The one who brightens each day for each and every one, would know so much, he thought!

'Oh please, I really want to learn from you,' Hanuman said, 'I will travel with you and face you while flying so that you can teach me as you travel. I will keep up with the speed of your chariot.'

'Will my glare not be uncomfortable for you?' Surya asked. 'I do not stop, not even for a moment. Will you not get tired?'

'I will willingly take all discomfort to learn from you,' Hanuman said.

Surya was touched by Hanuman's enthusiasm for learning. 'Then let us begin!' he said as he took him as his student.

In the thousands of years that followed, Hanuman kept pace with the chariot, facing the blindingly bright Surya. He learnt Sanskrit, its vocabulary, grammar and poetry; the Vedas and Puranas; how to change his size and weight as well as many other things from his guru. Hanuman was so focused that he remembered every word that Surya taught him.

Surya was mighty pleased with his student. 'Hanuman, you have always had wisdom. I just helped in opening the door to the wisdom you had. It is time now for you to return and reflect on what you have learnt.'

Hanuman used his hard-earned knowledge to help others, not to gain power or wealth.

Did you know?

Hanuman featured on the coins of several dynasties, including the Chandelas, Kalachuri, Hoysalas and Pandyas.

GANESHA
THE GOD OF KNOWLEDGE (NARA + GAJA)

SAMANVAYA

Ganesha is the wise, happy god who removes obstacles by using his intelligence. With his elephant head and human body, Ganesha symbolises the harmony between humans and animals, and that they can coexist peacefully.

Everyone, including all gods, invoke Ganesha before starting any task so that it can be completed smoothly.

Ganesha has the head of an elephant, and the wisdom, energy, power and strength of one, too. His big ears symbolize his ability to listen attentively to others' problems and offer wise solutions. He removes obstacles, like ignorance, fear and ego etc., and therefore brings happiness.

He has four hands and holds a shankha (conch), chakra (discus), paasha (noose) and a lotus in them. He has a big belly and loves eating laddoos. He rides a mouse. His strength comes from not harming anyone.

> Sushruta (6th century BCE), the father of surgery and author of the medical text Sushruta Samhita, would make small laddoos or balls of jaggery, sesame seeds and certain herbs along with honey as a medicinal supplement for his patients. Since then, laddoos have also become a delectable dessert.

Ganesha is the son of Parvati and Shiva and the brother of Kartikeya. He is married to Riddhi, who stands for material wealth, and Sidhhi, who stands for intellectual wealth and wisdom. He is the father of two sons Shubh (auspicious) and Laabh (profit). His daughter is Santoshi (satisfaction).

HINDU GODS AND GODDESSES

 Mooshak

 Pasha

 Ganesha Chaturthi

 Karpaka Vinayaka temple in Pillayarpatti, Tamil Nadu; Swayambhu Ganpati temple in Ganapatipule, Maharashtra

The rishi Vyasa had thought out the entire story of the Mahabharata, but he needed someone to write it down as he narrated it. Brahma said that Ganesha, the remover of obstacles with his wisdom, would be perfect. So, Vyasa narrated the story, and Ganesha wrote over days, weeks and years. One day as Ganesha was writing, his pen broke. Not wanting to stop, he broke off one of his tusks and used it as a pen! That is why you see him with a broken tusk!

When you use your intelligence and wisdom to get over all kinds of obstacles and spread positivity, you are Ganesha.

Did you know?

In 1893, the Maharashtrian freedom fighter Bal Gangadhar Tilak started the tradition of celebrating Ganesha Chaturthi as a community festival to bring people together and unite them against colonial rule.

GANESHA AND HIS MOOSHAK

Little Ganesha kept his parents on their toes. He would dart out of the house the second they got busy with other things and go around Mount Kailasa chasing butterflies, playing with birds, hiding behind trees until he was caught and dragged back home. It wasn't much easier when he was home either. Even as Parvati prepared a meal, little Ganesha would eat it all up, keeping Parvati busy in the cycle of cooking and feeding! And if there were laddoos being made, Parvati had to be even more on guard because Ganesha loved laddoos so much!

Shiva had to make extra effort to find a quiet place to sit in meditation. It wasn't easy—just as he was about to close his eyes, Ganesha would start giggling. The sound of his son's pure and innocent laughter would touch Shiva, and he would start laughing too!

Little Ganesha was a handful.

Kartikeya, unlike his brother Ganesha, was rather self-disciplined. He liked a sense of order around him and went about his tasks responsibly. He often went to convey his father's messages to different gods riding his Mayura (peacock).

Ganesha longed for a vaahana. It wasn't fair that Kartikeya had one and he did not. He had been asking his parents for so long, but they just would not listen to him.

One morning, Ganesha had been running around as usual and became rather tired. So when he saw Kartikeya leaving on his vaahana, he threw a fit.

'I want a vaahana too,' Ganesha said to Parvati, 'It is not fair that he gets one and I do not,' his lower lips quivered.

Parvati was sure that if they got a vaahana for Ganesha, it would mean yet another job for her. Keeping track of little

Ganesha was enough work, so she was in no mood to relent. 'You will get a vaahana when you can take care of it, Ganesha,' said Parvati giving him a laddoo.

Little Ganesha stomped his little feet. Big tears rolled down his eyes, and he started bawling. In between the tears, he took bites of the laddoo. It was delicious.

Shiva, who had just about closed his eyes to meditate, opened them again. 'Come here, my little boy,' he called.

Sniffling and nibbling on the laddoo, little Ganesha walked to Shiva. 'I have the perfect vaahana for you.'

Shiva closed his eyes and a mouse appeared in Ganesha's hands. He opened his eyes and said, 'This mooshak has been running around this entire place and nibbling on everything in this house for a long time now. The two of you will have a good time together.'

Ganesha was delighted. As soon as he put the mooshak down, it darted away. Ganesha darted behind. Shiva and Parvati smiled. Ganesha now had a task that would keep him busy!

DASHAAVATARA

Dashaavatara are the ten incarnations of Vishnu who come to earth to help in times of trouble and keep the world safe and in balance. These include various kinds of animals, humans from different walks of life and even creatures that are half-human and half-animal.

Divine forms that reflect the harmony between opposites—nature and spirit,

Dashaavatara (Purusha + Prakriti)
Matsya
Kurma
Varaaha
Narasimha
Vaamana
Parashurama
Rama
Krishna
Gautama
Kalki

MATSYA
THE FISH

Matsya is the first of the Dashaavatara or ten avatars of Vishnu. He is an enormous fish that can span the vastness of the entire cosmic ocean.

Matsya has the upper torso of a man and the lower body of a fish. His fish scales are radiant and shimmering. He is the saviour who bridges the aquatic and terrestrial realms, protecting and preserving life and knowledge.

Did you know?

There are a lot of similarities between the story of Noah's Ark and the story of Matsya.

 Vedanarayana temple or Matsya Narayana temple in Nagalapuram, Andhra Pradesh; Sri Matsya Narayana temple in Bengaluru, Karnataka

KING SATYAVRAT AND THE GROWING FISH

King Satyavrat was a generous king. He was also a sincere devotee. One day he was praying at the Kritmala river. As he cupped the water in his palms, a tiny fish swam in with it. The fish asked for the king's protection, saying the big fish would eat it. Kind-hearted Satyavrat placed the fish in his kamandala, waterpot, and returned home. In a day, the fish got too big for the kamandala, so Satyavrat got a bigger container. It took another day for the fish to become too big for that one, too. And so it went; each day, Satyavrat would get a larger and larger container, for the fish grew as big as the container it! Soon, the only place suitable for such a big fish was the vast sea.

As Satyavrat released the fish into the sea, it looked into his eyes, smiled and said, 'What if the big fish eat me, Satyavrat?'

In that moment Satyavrat saw Vishnu in Matsya.

'There will be a deluge on the seventh day from today that will destroy the world. You will find a huge boat on that day. Take the seeds of all plants and one male and female of each animal species and the Saptarishis, the seven great sages, on the boat. I will come to protect you all in this form.'

On the seventh day, Satyavrat sat in a boat with all the beings and seeds. The boat rocked furiously as the waters rose rapidly. Holding on tight to one another and the boat, Satyavrat thought of the fish, the matsya. It appeared that instant and brought the boat to safety.

Thus, Vishnu came as a matsya to save the world from chaos and ensure the continuity of life and knowledge.

Kurmanathaswamy temple in Srikurmam village, Andhra Pradesh; Gavi Ranganatha Swamy temple in Gavi Rangapura, Karnataka

KURMA
THE TURTLE

Kurma is the second of avatar of Vishnu. He is an enormous turtle who provides a strong, stable foundation that can balance the huge Mount Sumeru or Meru on its back so as to churn the ocean.

Kurmaasana is a seated yoga posture where you arrange your body so that it resembles a turtle's. The arms and legs are stretched out and the torso rests on the floor in a forward fold. The back resembles the shell of the turtle.

The Kurma avatar shows the importance of perseverance and cooperation between opposing forces to achieve a common goal.

Did you know?

Leatherbacks are the biggest turtles in the world. They can grow up to seven feet in length and weigh more than 900 kgs! They are the last survivors of a family of turtles that has existed for more than 100 million years.

 Bhu Varahaswamy Temple in Tirupati, Andhra Pradesh; Varaha Temple in Pushkar, Rajasthan

VARAAHA
THE BOAR

DASHAAVATARA

Varaaha is the third avatar of Vishnu. He is a colossal, robust, muscular boar with a prominent snout and huge tusks. He has the strength and ability to root through the earth. He is ferocious to all evil and kind to the rest. He wears fine necklaces, earrings and a crown.

Varaaha rescued Prithvi (Earth) from the depths of the cosmic ocean, lifting her with his tusks from where she was submerged by Hiranyaaksha. He dispels chaos, retrieves hidden treasures, restores order and supports life.

Did you know?

The tusks of boars are their elongated canine teeth. Boars are also excellent swimmers.

 Simhachalam Narasimha temple in Visakhapatnam, Andhra Pradesh; Yadadri temple in Yadagirigutta and Hemachala Lakshmi Narasimha Swamy temple in Mallur, Telangana

 Narasimha Jayanti

NARASIMHA
THE MAN-LION

Narasimha is the fourth of Vishnu's Dashaavataras. He has the head of a lion and the body of a human.

This huge avatar has the head of a lion, with a wild mane, sharp teeth and claws and fierce, glowing eyes. He has a strong, muscular human body and is dressed in fine garments and jewellery. He protects the kind and punishes the evil.

Narasimha symbolises victory over persecution and destruction of evil.

> In the classical dance form of Kathakali, the story of Narasimha and Hiranyakashipu is often performed.

DASHAAVATARA

Did you know?
Several kings of the Gupta Empire minted coins that featured images of Narasimha.

PRAHALADA'S DEVOTION

Jaya and Vijaya were the formidable and loyal gatekeepers of Vaikuntha, where Vishnu lives. They were particular about not disturbing Vishnu when he was resting.

One day, the four sons of Brahma arrived at Vaikuntha, but Jaya and Vijaya refused them entry as Vishnu was sleeping. Furious with the guards' audacity, the sons of Brahma cursed them to be born on earth.

Vijaya and Jaya pleaded for the curse to be undone, and even Vishnu tried to intervene, but the curse was irrevocable. Jaya and Vijaya were born as Hiranyakashipu and Hiranyaaksha.

Hiranyaaksha won a boon from Brahma that made him invincible. No being, whether divine or mortal, would be able to cause his death. He then went all out to hurt and harass people on earth. Vishnu came as Varaaha to rid the earth of him. (Read the story on …)

Meanwhile Hiranyakashipu had also pleased Brahma with his devotion. He had prayed for years together, unbothered as anthills and creepers grew over him.

At long last, Brahma appeared before him. 'Ask what you wish for, Hiranyakashipu,' he said.

'Lord, please bless me so that I can be killed neither by humans nor by animals or devils, neither during day nor night, neither outside nor inside, neither by wood, metal or stone, neither on earth nor in the sky.'

Brahma granted him the wish. 'Tathaastu,' he said, and vanished.

With each passing day Hiranyakashipu's arrogance grew. He felt more and more powerful and became less and less patient, kind and gracious.

He wanted to see his son Prahalad rule as ruthlessly as he did, but Prahalad seemed to have crazy thoughts.

When Hiranyakashipu had asked Prahalad what he wished for, the boy had said he wanted to be devoted to Vishnu.

Vishnu?

'The same Vishnu who came as Varaaha to kill your uncle? You want to pray to that Vishnu?!' he raged.

Prahalad was sent away with the hope that he would return as a strong, focused asura ready to follow the ideals of Hiranyakashipu.

But nothing changed in Prahalad. No matter how much he was scolded or caned, Vishnu's name remained on his lips and Vishnu remained his ideal. Hiranyakashipu raged more and more with each passing day.

He ordered that Prahalad's hands be tied behind his back and that he be pushed down from the highest mountain. His servants followed the orders without a single mistake. But with Vishnu in his heart, Prahalad happily rolled down the mountain without a single scratch.

Hiranyakashipu ordered that Prahalad be drowned. But seeing Vishnu in his heart, the waves lifted and gently placed the boy on the shore.

Hiranyakashipu then ordered Prahalad's sweet to be poisoned. But the poison turned to sugar!

Next, poisonous snakes were released around Prahalad. The snakes raised their hoods above his head and made Prahalad look like Shiva himself.

Hiranyakashipu ordered that Prahalad be thrown in front of a mad elephant. Lying in its path, Prahalad looked up at the elephant. The elephant lowered its head, and lifting Prahalad with his trunk, placed him on its back.

Hiranyakashipu was at his wit's end! He had tried what felt like a hundred different ways to get Prahalad to stop taking Vishnu's name, but that had failed. He had tried a thousand ways to get rid of Prahalad, but that had failed even more spectacularly!

Hiranyakashipu called his sister Holika for help. Holika had a shawl that protected everything under it from fire. She wrapped the shawl around herself, then held Prahalad in her lap. Hiranyakashipu's men lit a fire around them.

As always, Vishnu lived in Prahalad's heart. Just as the fire was began to blaze, the shawl swiftly moved from Holika to Prahalad. Holika was reduced to ashes in an instant, but Prahalad remained unhurt.

Hiranyakashipu was beyond angry!

He dragged Prahalad to the centre of the hall. 'Where is this Vishnu you always talk about? What does he do for you? What has he done for you that you disregard your own father? You sing praises of this Vishnu that no one can even see! Where is he now?' Hiranyakashipu thundered, his face burning with anger.

'He is everywhere, father,' said Prahalad calmly.

'Everywhere? You say everywhere? Then he should be in this pillar right in front of you!' Hiranyakashipu screamed, throwing his mace at it.

The pillar cracked and broke open with the blow.

Out stepped a huge creature no one had ever seen. He had the head of a lion and the body of a man, and had big, sharp teeth and big, sharp claws. He was Narasimha, the fourth avatar of Vishnu.

He was neither human nor animal or devil. It was neither day nor night.

Narasimha picked up Hiranyakashipu with one hand and dragged him to the door. He sat down on the threshold and placed Hiranyakashipu on his lap.

Hiranyakashipu was neither outside nor inside. He was neither on earth nor in the sky.

Narasimha tore Hiranyakashipu apart with his long, sharp frightful claws.

He was killed neither by wood, metal nor stone.

Narasimha roared furiously. Brahma, Shiva and Lakshmi tried to calm him down, but he paced up and down, furious at the havoc Hiranyakashipu had unleashed. He finally calmed down when Prahalad went to him.

Did you know?

Ahobilam in Andhra Pradesh is believed to be the site where Lord Narasimha vanquished Hiranyakashipu, protecting Prahalada.

Thrikkakara Vamanamoorthy temple in Thrikkakara, Kerala; Sri Thiruvikrama Perumal temple, Sirkazhi, Tamil Nadu

VAAMANA
THE DWARF

Vaamana is the fifth avatar of Vishnu. He is a humble dwarf with a calm, gentle, radiant expression. He wears a dhoti and a sacred thread across his chest. His hair is tied in a top knot. He carries a danda (wooden staff), kamandala (water pot) and an umbrella. He has small feet and often goes barefoot.

Vaamana represents humility, righteousness and divinity in the most unassuming forms. His initial small stature represents modesty and simplicity, while his later cosmic form underscores Vishnu's supreme power and ability to restore cosmic order.

THREE STEPS' WORTH OF LAND

Bali was the grandson of Prahalad. He was an exceptional king. There was no poverty or crime under his rule. He was adored by his people. He had such good relationships with everyone that it made the devas insecure. Indra begged Vishnu to do something so that Bali would go away.

Vishnu took the avatar of a vaamana, a dwarf, and visited Bali when he was conducting a yagna. Like a gracious host, Bali welcomed him and asked if he had any requests.

'Can I get three steps' worth of land?' the vaamana asked.

Looking at his size, Bali was slightly amused. His request was modest, Bali thought, and said, 'Yes, absolutely!'

Bali's guru, Shukracharya realised that the dwarf was not who he appeared to be, but before he could tell Bali, the king had agreed to the seemingly small request. As soon as Bali said yes, the vaamana started to grow. Soon, a gigantic form spanning the universe stood before the king.

With his first step, he covered the earth. With his second step, he covered the heavens. With no place left for the third, Bali came forward and offered his head as the resting place for the third step.

Touched by Bali's devotion and humility, the 'vaamana' blessed him and asked him to rule the netherworld, granting him immortality and a place in the pantheon of revered beings. It was also decided that Bali would visit his people once every year. That visit is celebrated as Onam. The place where this incident is believed to have occurred is Thrikkakara in Kochi, Kerala, where the Thrikkakara Vamanamoorthy temple has been built.

PARASHURAMA
THE ANGRY WARRIOR

Parashurama is the sixth avatar of Vishnu. He is a sage warrior who safeguards dharma and appears to put an end to corrupt, cruel, unjust rulers and warriors.

He is strong, short tempered and always ready for a battle in pursuit of justice. His posture reflects his warrior nature. He is fuelled by his fury. He has a long, flowing beard; his hair is tied in a top knot and he wears a dhoti. His eyes reflect his determination and focus. He is an expert at martial arts and has a thorough knowledge of all kinds of weapons and their use. He carries a parashu, a battle axe, the most lethal close-combat weapon in the epics given to him by Shiva. Parashurama will train Kalki, the tenth avatar of Vishnu in martial arts and weaponry.

> Legend has it that Parashurama founded Kalaripayattu, the ancient martial art and believed to be among the oldest surviving martial arts of the world.

Did you know?
Parashurama was the guru of Dronacharya, who taught the Pandavas and Kauravas.

 Parashu

 Parashuram temple in Chiplun, Maharashtra; Sree Parasurama temple in Thiruvallam, Kerala

 Parashuram Dvadashi

PARASHURAMA AND SHIVA'S BOW

It was the day of the swayamvara; grand preparations had been made. Sita, the princess of Mithila, was going to choose her life partner.

King Janaka, her father, had set a condition that the man who could string Pinaaka, the mighty bow of Shiva, would marry Sita. Sita had a lot of suitors; princes had come from near and far in the hope of marrying her. One after the other they came to show their strength, but they could not even lift the bow.

Rama, the seventh avatar of Vishnu, had come with his brother Lakshmana and the sage Vishwamitra to the ceremony. When it was his turn, he walked towards the bow, bowed his head in respect to Shiva and effortlessly lifted and strung it.

A bow works best when its string is tight. Rama stretched the bowstring to test its tautness. But as he pulled the string, the bow broke into two with a thunderous crack. The earth trembled, and a hush fell over the court full of people.

The sound of Pinaaka breaking was so loud, it reached Parashurama. The warrior sage was furious. He saw it as a sign of disrespect to Shiva, as well as a challenge to his own strength and prowess, a personal insult.

Wielding his parashu, he arrived at the court of King Janaka. Parashurama's arrival sent a shudder among all those at the court. He was burning with rage. 'Who has dared to break this bow? Speak up! Your end is certain,' he thundered.

Lakshmana, with the instincts of a kshatriya, a warrior, was not intimidated by Parashurama. He found it amusing at first,

but when there seemed no end to Parashurama's fury, he was eager to challenge him.

But before Lakshmana could do anything, Rama spoke up respectfully and calmly, 'I am the one who unintentionally broke the bow.'

Parashurama dripped with rage. 'Who do you think you are to break Pinaaka? You think you are a great warrior? I have put thousands like you to rest because of the arrogance of you kshatriyas. Here, take this bow I hold. It is Shaaranga, the bow of Vishnu. Let's see if you can string this,' he challenged.

Rama stepped up respectfully. He took the bow and strung it effortlessly. 'Where should I release the arrow, Sir?' he asked.

Parashurama could not believe it! How could it be so easy for Rama? He realised that Rama was Vishnu's avatar, and understood that his own role in the divine plan was complete. He bowed to Rama, acknowledging his superiority and the continuation of Vishnu's mission to uphold dharma in the world.

RAMA
THE PERFECT MAN

DASHAAVATARA

Rama is the seventh of the Dashaavatara. He is the perfect, son, brother, husband and king. He is the protector of dharma, as he upholds social values and follows rules. He is committed to truth and justice.

Rama is young, radiant and handsome. He has big, expressive eyes and a mesmerising smile. He has a kshatriya's physique and a royal demeanour. He is calm, compassionate and patient, determined, brave, intelligent and humble. He carries Shaaranga, Vishnu's bow, and a quiver of arrows.

He is the crown prince of Ayodhya, the eldest son of King Dasharatha. His mother is Queen Kaushalya. He is the brother of Bharata, Lakshmana and Shatrughna. He is the husband of Sita and the father of Luv and Kush.

Rama is the hero of Valmiki's epic Ramayana.

> Ramayana was originally written in Sanskrit, but almost every part of the country has its own version, written in the regional language. There are even versions of the Ramayana in southeast Asian countries such as Thailand, Vietnam and the Maldives.
>
> Rama's reign in Ayodhya, known as Ramarajya, is considered to be a state of perfect social harmony, economic justice and political freedom.
>
> The Ramayana mentions several rivers, including Sarayu, Ganga, Yamuna, Mandakini and Gomti. Can you mark these on a map?

 Shaaranga

 Ram Navami, Dussehra, Diwali

 Ram Mandir in Ayodhya, Uttar Pradesh; Ram Raja temple in Orchcha, Madhya Pradesh; Triprayar Sri Rama temple in Thrissur, Kerala; Sita Ramachandraswamy temple in Telangana

RAMA AND THE KEVAT

Rama, the son of King Dasharatha and Queen Kaushalya, was a role model for his younger brothers Bharata, Lakshmana and Shatrughna. He was loved by all for his kindness, his skills in archery, and his all-round knowledge.

Soon, the time came for King Dasharatha to crown Rama as king. But before the king could make that announcement, Queen Kaikeyi reminded him of a promise he had made to her. 'You promised me two boons. I ask that my son Bharata be crowned king and Rama be banished to the forest for fourteen years.'

Dasharatha was completely heartbroken, but a promise was a promise.

Rama, always obedient, said, 'I will honour your word, father. I will go to the forest for fourteen years.' Sita and Lakshmana insisted on joining him. 'We will not let you face this alone,' they said.

The people of Ayodhya wept as they watched their beloved crown prince, his wife and his brother leave for the forest. Rama, Sita and Lakshmana walked long distances crossing villages and towns.

'Who are you travellers? Where are you from and why are you going?' curious villagers asked.

'We are from Ayodhya, the kingdom of Dasharatha. We are his sons, following our mother's orders,' Rama replied.

'Which of these is your husband and which your brother-in-law?' they asked Sita.

'The dark one is my husband, the fair one is my brother-in-law,' said Sita smiling.

On their way they met a tribal chieftain named Guha and requested him to arrange for a kevat, a boatsman, to cross the Ganga. That day there was only one boat by the river.

Guha sent for the kevat and asked him to take the three across the river. 'I will not let them step on my boat till Rama allows me to wash his feet,' said the kevat.

Guha knitted his brows, 'How are the two things linked?'

'I have heard that a big rock transformed into a woman when the dust of his foot touched it! I am a poor man, I have only one boat. It is made of wood and not as hard as that stone. What if my boat turns into a woman too? I will lose the only means I have of earning money and will have to find a way of feeding that woman too! I cannot risk it. I will take them across only if he allows me to wash his feet,' elaborated the boatsman.

Guha was touched by such innocence. Rama smiled and agreed to his feet being washed.

The kevat brought a small plate, crouched near Rama and asked him to step into it. But the plate was small; after he placed his right foot, there wasn't enough place for Rama to put his left foot in. 'Place your hand on my head to balance yourself,' suggested the boatsman.

As soon as Rama followed the suggestion, the kevat was overwhelmed—and Rama knew why. The kevat had planned all this so he could be blessed by Rama.

He then ferried the three across the river.

As they got off the boat, Rama looked around to see what he could give to the kevat for his service. Sita understood. She took off a ring and handed it to Rama.

Rama offered the ring to the boatsman, but he refused to take it. 'We don't pay each other, being in the same profession.'

'Same profession? How are we in the same profession?'

The kevat smiled, 'I ferry people across the river. You ferry people across the ocean of life. Are we not in the same profession?'

KRISHNA
THE PLAYFUL ONE

Krishna is the eighth of Vishnu's ten avatars. He came on earth to end the tyranny and cruelty of rulers like Kansa and to restore dharma, righteousness, order and peace, and to protect the innocent and punish the cruel.

Krishna has dark blue skin (reflecting the colour of the cosmos), a mesmerizing smile and sparkling eyes reflecting compassion and mischief. He has curly black hair. He is a playful, mischievous child, an adventurous youth, a charming man and a valued teacher. He plays the flute and takes cows for grazing. He wears a crown and has a peacock feather tucked in it.

There are thousands of stories about Krishna's love for all dairy products. So great is his love for butter that he is called 'maakhan chor' (butter thief in Hindi), because he would sneak into houses and steal butter with his friends!

Krishna is the son of Vasudeva, the king of Vrishnis, and Devaki, the sister of Kansa, and was born in Mathura. He was brought up by Yashoda and Nanda in Gokul. His older brother is Balarama and his sister is Subhadra. He is the cousin of the Pandavas. He is the closest friend of Radha, the husband of Rukmini and the wise charioteer of Arjuna in the Mahabharata.

Krishna was the eighth child of Devaki and Vasudeva. Devaki's brother Kansa, the evil king of Mathura had been warned by a prophecy that he would be killed by the eighth child of his sister. To prevent this prophecy from coming true, Kansa imprisoned Devaki and Vasudeva.

Krishna was born in jail at midnight amid thunder, lightning and heavy rain. Just as he was born, a divine voice told Vasudeva

 Sudarshana Chakra

 Venu/Bansi

 Janamshtmi, Dahi Handi, Holi

 Dwarkadhish temple in Dwarka, Gujrat; Shree Jagannatha temple in Puri, Odisha; Radha Rama temple in Vrindavan, Uttar Pradesh

to take the newborn to Gokul, a village on the banks of the Yamuna, leave the child in the house of Yashoda and Nanda and return immediately with their newborn. The prison doors magically opened, the Yamuna magically parted to give way and Vasudeva crossed the river with Krishna in heavy rainfall. Krishna grew up in Gokul and had many adventures. Eventually he returned to Mathura and killed Kansa, fulfilling the prophecy.

Krishna has many names. As Madhava he is delightful, as Mohana he is the enchanter, as Gopala he is protector of the cows, as Govinda he is the chief herdsman, as Jagannatha, he is lord of the universe. He brings together unconditional love, mischief, knowledge and wisdom.

Did you know?

Mahabalipuram has Krishna's butterball. Legend is that this ball of butter, fell from heaven. The rock is 20 feet high and 5 metres wide and stands on a slippery slope of a hill defying gravity!

DAIRY LOVE

Little Krishna loved milk, butter and yogurt. From the day he started crawling, he set out to find the earthen pots full of fresh creamy butter and yogurt that his mother Yashoda made every day. Yashoda's friends said they hadn't seen any toddler crawl as fast as him—and with such determination and mischief in his eyes!

Indeed, Kanha (another name for Krishna) crawled faster than they could run. By the time they reached the pots, Kanha would have already enjoyed a few handfuls of butter and yogurt. They always found him content and happy, sporting a broad toothless grin, with butter and yogurt smeared all over his face and hands.

When he began walking, the pots of yogurt and butter in the entire neighbourhood came under threat. He would sneak into homes and wait until no one was near the pots. Nimble-footed Kanha would then dart towards the pots and eat to his hearts content.

People started calling him 'maakhan chor' (butter thief). Yashoda was tired of the complaints she got from the neighbourhood. No amount of anger or cajoling helped. Whenever she got angry, Kanha spoke with such innocence and with so much love that her heart melted. He continued to get away with his pranks.

Helpless in managing the maakhan chor, the women came together to brainstorm.

'What can we do with this boy? He polishes off all the butter in the pot and walks about so innocently that it feels wrong to say anything to him,' a neighbour said.

'Yes, I didn't realise that the yogurt pot was empty till late last evening! He leaves the pots as if they were untouched, and just when you think your yogurt was safe from little Kanha, you open the pot to see it was not!' said another.

'I have tried keeping the pots at different places, but he finds out somehow!' said another exasperatedly.

'How about we hang our pots way higher than his reach?' said Yashoda.

'That could work!' her friends spoke almost in chorus.

'Let's work on that then. Don't say a word to anyone. Just get everything ready so you can hang the pots high enough for you to reach, but not him. Tomorrow morning our little maakhan chor will be in for a surprise,' Yashoda said, a mischievous smile dancing on her lips.

Next morning all those who had churned fresh butter and made yogurt moved about with a smile that held a common secret. Pots hung beautifully down from ceilings, enticing elegantly.

When little Kanha walked about after his morning play, there were no pots to be found at their usual spot. Instead, they hung high above, out of his reach!

'It would need five of me to get to those pots!' exclaimed Kanha, his face falling at the realisation.

He took out his flute and played his favourite tune. It always cleared his mind. It also served as a signal to all his friends to get together to play.

His smile was back, as was the mischief in his eyes.

Within a minute all his friends had gathered.

'Kanha, we just got home after playing all morning! What's up?' asked a friend who'd sped his way and stood panting.

'We have a task at hand! It's time for teamwork, coordination, trust and action. Let's go to my house,' Kanha said, and off they went to stand below a pot of yogurt.

The boys huddled together, arms around each other's shoulders, bobbing their heads in agreement.

When they separated, the tallest boys stood in a circle. The shorter ones then climbed on their tall friends' shoulders, and in this way built a human pyramid!

Kanha climbed up the four levels of the human pyramid and reached the pot! He broke the pot with his fist, and yummy, delightful fresh yogurt spilled out! There was joy and laughter as the boys slurped yogurt off their arms and faces.

Yashoda had been watching the boys form a human pyramid from a window. There was love in her eyes and admiration for how they got together for a common goal.

Ever since then, many people across India recreate this incident on or a day after Janamashtmi. Called Dahi Handi (literally, pot of yogurt), people form human pyramids to reach and break pots of yogurt hanging from great heights.

> Dahi Handi is a competitive event in many parts of India and teams prepare for months. Those participating are called Govinda, another name for Krishna.

GAUTAMA BUDDHA
THE WISE ONE

Siddhartha Gautama, known as the Buddha, is the ninth avatar of Vishnu and lived about 2,500 years ago. He was a kind and wise teacher who wanted to help people live better lives. He taught them to be compassionate and non-violent. He showed them a better way to live by focusing on being good, following dharma—doing the right things—and correcting excessive rituals and animal sacrifices.

Siddhartha was born a prince in Lumbini (in Nepal) to King Shuddhodana and Queen Maya. Sadly, his mother passed away just days after he was born. Astrologers predicted that Siddhartha would either become a great king or a great monk. His father wanted him to be a king, so he gave Siddhartha a luxurious life and shielded him from anything sad or bad, like old age, sickness or death.

At sixteen, Siddhartha married a beautiful princess named Yashodhara. But when he turned twenty-nine, everything changed. He wanted to see the city. His father allowed it, but he made sure to hide all the sick and old people. However, they missed one old man. When Siddhartha saw him, he learned that everyone, including himself and his father, would grow old one day.

On his next three trips outside the palace, he saw a sick person, a dead body as well as a peaceful person meditating under a tree. These sights made Siddhartha want to leave the city and find a way to overcome these sufferings.

His father offered him all kinds of things to stay, but Siddhartha refused. He wanted to find a way to never get sick,

 Mahabodhi temple in Bodh Gaya, Bihar; Mahaparinirvana temple in Kushinagar and Sarnath Buddha temple in Sarnath, Uttar Pradesh

 Buddha Purnima

grow old or die. When his father said that this was impossible, Siddhartha decided to leave. He took one last look at his sleeping wife and baby son before leaving.

Siddhartha left his royal life. He cut off his hair, changed into simple clothes and started living in the forest. He ate whatever people gave him in his begging bowl and searched for a way to go beyond birth and death.

For the next six years, he practised meditation and learned from many teachers. He mastered their teachings but realised they wouldn't stop the cycle of rebirth. He then joined five ascetics who believed that extreme self-punishment would lead to enlightenment. Siddhartha tried this too, eating only one pea a day.

But he soon understood that punishing his body wasn't the answer. He accepted a dish of rice from a young woman, regaining his strength. His five companions thought he had given up and left him. Alone, Siddhartha vowed to sit under a bodhi (peepul/sacred fig) tree until he discovered the truth beyond birth and death.

> Krishna says that among trees he is ashvatha. It is the Sanskrit name of the peepul.

He meditated from morning till night, and from night until day. No matter the temptation, Siddhartha spent six years like this. Mara, the god of desire, tried to disturb him with storms and temptations, but Siddhartha stayed calm, meditating on love. He turned Mara's attacks into harmless flowers. Mara's three daughters, Lust, Thirst and Discontent, also failed to distract him. Finally, Mara claimed the ground Siddhartha sat on, but Siddhartha touched the earth, asking it to witness his right to sit there. The earth responded with a tremor, and Mara left.

That full-moon night in May, Siddhartha had deep realisations. He remembered all his past lives, understood the cycle of rebirth and learned about the truth of suffering, its cause, its end and the path to end it. By morning, he had achieved enlightenment and became the Buddha, the awakened one.

The Buddha stayed near the Bodhi tree for seven weeks thinking about his enlightenment. During a rainy week, a serpent king shielded him from the storm. After this, two merchants offered him honey and cakes. The gods provided a bowl, and the Buddha received the food. In return, he gave the merchants some of his hair.

Unsure how to share his understanding, the Buddha was encouraged by Brahma, the god of creation, to teach. He thought of his five ascetic companions and found them in a deer park in Sarnath. They doubted him at first but were drawn to his presence. The Buddha taught them all that he had learned—about the middle way between self-indulgence and self-punishment, how to live an ideal life, and to go beyond the endless cycle of suffering, and life and death.

The five ascetics became the first members of the sangha, the community of monks, and achieved enlightenment. As the Buddha's fame grew, many others joined the sangha, including his wife Yashodhara and his son Rahula, who became a monk.

The Buddha travelled across northeastern India, teaching dharma. He emphasised the middle way, ethical conduct, meditation and wisdom. His teachings attracted followers from all over the world, and that is how the religion of Buddhism was born. He died in Kushinagar, in modern-day Uttar Pradesh.

The place where Siddhartha became the Buddha under the peepul tree is Bodh Gaya, in modern-day Bihar.

KALKI
THE ONE YET TO COME

Kalki is the last of the Dashaavatara. He will appear to end Kaliyuga, a dark, destructive, corrupt, chaotic period, to bring back dharma into the world and thus usher in a Sat yuga, starting a new cycle of time.

Kalki rides Devadatta, a majestic white horse. He holds the gleaming sword called Ratnamaru in his right hand and moves like a blazing comet. The handle of his sword has jewels on it. He is trained in warfare by Parashurama. He has a parrot that knows the past, present and future. Yuga is a period of time that spans many, many centuries. There are four yugas, and they keep repeating in a cycle. With each yuga, the dharma in the world keeps reducing.

Yuga	Duration	Vishnu avatar	Dharma
Sat	432,000x 4 years	Matsya, Kurma, Varaha, Narasimha	●
Treta	432,000 x 3 years	Vaamana, Parashurama, Rama	◕
Dvaapara	432,000x 2 years	Krishna	◐
Kali	432,000 years	Buddha	◔

 Ratnamaru

 Kalki Jayanti

 Kalki Mandir in Jaipur, Rajasthan

HARIHARA
VISHNU + SHIVA

Harihara is the combined form of Vishnu (Hari) and Shiva (Hara), the harmonious, symphonic coexistence of seemingly opposing energies. This form is also known as Shankaranarayana.

The deity symbolises the unity and harmony between these two powerful gods, showing that preservation and destruction are both essential parts of life. The deity is depicted rather literally as the combination of the two gods. One side of Harihara is Shiva, covered in ashes, dressed in hide, wearing a jatamukuta (crown of dreadlocks) and holding his trishula. The other side is the blue-skinned Vishnu, dressed in yellow silken garments and holding his chakra and shankha.

> The city of Haridwar is also known as Haradwar, because it serves as the dwar (gateway) to Badrinath (Hari or Vishnu's home) and Kedarnath (Hara or Shiva's home).

Did you know?
Harihara came into being to bring the devotees of Shiva and Vishnu together, and to show how the two complement each other.

 Trishula and Chakra

 Harihareshwara temple in Harihar, Karnataka

THE BIRTH OF HARIHARA

Guhasura ruled over Guharanya, but the asura wanted more. He prayed to Brahma for years. Pleased by his devotion, Brahma appeared in front of Guhasura.

'Ask what you wish for,' Brahma said.

'Grant me a boon, so that I cannot be killed by humans, devas, Shiva or Vishnu,' said Guhasura.

'Tathaastu,' said Brahma, granting the boon.

Guhasura then went on a rampage, made confident by his newfound boon, spreading fear and suffering. There was no peace for living beings near him, and there was no way to stop him,

Humans and devas ran to Vishnu and Shiva for help, but what could they do? Brahma's boon had been granted, and there was no way to undo it.

Even so, it was necessary to put an end to Guhasura's evil intentions and actions.

Vishnu and Shiva thought hard. They would need their combined energies to face Guhasura. They decided to merge their energies and their forms to take the form of Harihara. With the combined energies of Vishnu and Shiva, Harihara descended upon Guharanya. A fierce battle followed, but in the end, Harihara emerged victorious, and peace was restored in Guharanya.

Trishula

Ardhanareeswarar temple in Tiruchengode, Tamil Nadu

ARDHANAREESHVARA
NAARI + NARA

Ardhanareeshvara is the combined form of Shiva and Parvati in one body. The form shows that both male and female energies are equally important for a happy and balanced life. So, Ardhanareeshvara is the combined form of the masculine and feminine energies in one being. The left side is Parvati with her hair tied, bindi, breast, garments, anklet and foot tinted in red with aalta. The right side is Shiva, with his matted locks and three eyes, dressed in hide, a crescent moon in his hair and serpent around his neck.

Ardhanareeshvara reflects that Shakti (female) and Shiva (male) are equals, necessary, complement each other and together make one whole.

Did you know?
Aalta (also known as mahavar) was traditionally made by soaking betel leaves and lac.

A LESSON FOR BHRIGU

Bhrigu was a sincere devotee of Shiva. He only wanted to worship Shiva. He began his day by performing a parikrama of Shiva. Parvati and Shiva were always together, but Bhrigu found ways of leaving Parvati out of his prayers.

When Shiva and Parvati stood together, Bhrigu would ask her to move so he could go around Shiva before he began his day. Shiva was amused by Bhrigu and by Parvati's annoyance.

One morning, when Shiva saw Bhrigu walking towards him, he asked Parvati to sit on his lap. When Bhrigu saw Parvati sitting on Shiva's lap he realised that if he did a parikrama, it would include Parvati.

The sage turned himself into a bee and went just around Shiva. Parvati was so annoyed that the next morning, she looked at Shiva and the two merged into one.

Bhrigu understood that Shakti and Shiva are one, and any attempt to see them as separate is futile.

Did you know?

Parikrama means to circumambulate. That is, move in a clockwise direction around a deity or sacred object that is to the right of the worshipper?

SAMUDRAMANTHANA
CHURNING OF THE OCEAN

Samudramanthana, the churning of the ocean, is an event that reflects the unity of devas and daanavas, maanavas and pashus who come together to find the pot of amrita, the nectar of immortality, by churning the vast ocean.

The churning or manthana of the samudra, the ocean, was underway. It had brought the Devas, the gods, and Daanavas, the demons, together. Everyone wanted a share of amrita, the magical drink that turned its drinkers immortal, but it lay deep in the ocean along with many other treasures. Getting the amrita was a huge task and could only be done when everyone worked together.

Sumeru Parvat, also known as Mount Meru, stood at the centre of the ocean, where it would be used as a churning stick. Vasuki, the king of serpents, was coiled around the mountain, acting as the churning rope for the great cosmic event.

The devas held Vasuki's tail, the daanavas the head. By turns, the devas and daanavas pulled Vasuki towards them. This ended up rotating Sumeru Parvat in both directions, churning the ocean. But Meru's own weight and the force with which the ocean was churned was so great that the mountain began to sink. Panic spread like wildfire until Vishnu took charge of the situation. He decided to take the form of a kurma, a turtle. Kurma supported Meru on its back, keeping the mountain afloat. The churning resumed with renewed energy.

Excitement was in the air!

The first thing that appeared was Halaahala, a poison so powerful that it could destroy all creation. Panic rose. The devas and daanavas ran to Shiva for help.

Shiva appeared and calmly drank up the Halaahala, but his throat began to turn blue from the poison. An alarmed Parvati grabbed Shiva's throat and pressed hard to stop the poison from going further down. And this is how Shiva's throat turned blue and he got the name Neelakantha (blue throat).

The churning resumed now that the Halaahala had been dealt with. The devas and daanavas churned for over a thousand years. And from that hard work, fourteen other treasures emerged.

The rishis took Kaamadhenu, the wish-fulfilling white cow. They wanted the mother of all cows so that she could bless them with abundant milk and ghee needed for their yagnas.

Uchchaishravas, the radiant, flying white horse with seven heads arose from the waves. He was taken by Bali, and later by Indra in another incident.

Airavata, the graceful white elephant with four tusks emerged. Indra took this king of elephants as his vaahana.

Vishnu claimed the Kaustubha, the most precious gem in existence.

Kalpavriksha, the wish-fulfilling tree with blossoms that never wilt emerged. The Devas took it to Indraloka.

Paarijata, the flowering tree, came next.

Paarijata is known by many other names, for instance, harshringar, shefali, shiuli in Hindi and Bangla. In English, it is known as night-blooming jasmine and coral jasmine. It is said to have medicinal properties.

Then appeared Lakshmi, the goddess of wealth, dressed in silk and laden with jewellery. She chose Vishnu as her partner. Vaaruni, the goddess of wine, also called Sura, emerged with the drink in hand. The daanavas were delighted with her company.

Chandra appeared from the frolicking waves. Shiva placed him as a crescent in his hair.

Paanchajanya, the shankha (conch) symbolising the five elements of nature and the sound of creation appeared. It was claimed by Vishnu.

Apsaras, elegant and graceful dancers, emerged from the ocean. They graced Indra's court as the royal dancers.

Vishnu took the bow named Shaaranga. Several of his avatars—Parashurama, Rama and Krishna—carried it.

Then, a handsome, young, well-built man walked out of the ocean. Dhanvantari became the celestial doctor. He had bluish skin and pinkish eyes. Black curly locks fell on his broad shoulders, and he wore fine jewellery. In his hands was the pot of Amrita.

The sight of the amrita got everyone in a frenzy. Both the devas and daanavas wanted it desperately—and as desperately wanted to keep it away from one another.

Their joint effort for obtaining the amrita was quickly forgotten. A massive fight erupted. Both parties forcefully pushed and pulled at one another and Dhanvantari in hopes of snatching the pot. In the process, a few drops of amrita sloshed out and fell on Prayag in Uttar Pradesh, Haridwar in Uttarakhand, Ujjain in Madhya Pradesh and Nasik in Maharashtra. That is why the Kumbh Mela is held in these places.

The daanavas were faster and managed to snatch the amrita. However, their joy was short-lived; they began to fight among themselves. The yelling was deafening.

The devas looked on helplessly at the scene, not knowing what to do! Fortunately, Vishnu decided to help. He took the form of Mohini, a beautiful woman.

The appearance of Mohini brought great relief to the devas. A smile broke on their lips.

Mohini smiled as she walked towards the squabbling daanavas. A hush fell over the group, so stunned were they by her beauty.

'Allow me to distribute this amrita to all of you,' Mohini said, extending her hand for the pot.

Mesmerised by Mohini's voice and demeanour, the daanavas handed it over.

'Please, may I have the devas on one side and the daanavas on the other? I will distribute the amrita by turns, one by one.'

Everyone complied eagerly and without question. But something felt off to the daanava Svarbhanu. He decided to disguise himself and sit among the devas.

Mohini began to serve the amrita. The devas and daanavas both looked to be enjoying the drink. But the enchanting Mohini had a trick up her sleeve: she was giving the amrita to the devas and liquor to the daanavas!

It was Svarbhanu's turn to receive the amrita. As Mohini began to ladle it out, Surya and Chandra, who were sitting beside the daanava, realised his true identity.

As soon as they raised the alarm, Mohini turned into Vishnu and threw his Sudarshana Chakra at the daanava. Svarbhanu's head was severed from his body. But because he had consumed the amrita, both parts survived.

Since then, the head is known as Rahu, and the torso is known as Ketu. Because Brahma had agreed to give Svarbhanu the status of a planet, after this incident Rahu and Ketu came to be a part of the Navagraha, the nine planetary deities. Rahu and Ketu have a strained relationship with Surya and Chandra and run behind them to swallow them. When they manage to swallow Surya, we have a solar eclipse; and when they swallow Chandra, we have a lunar eclipse.

GLOSSARY

Adharma: Unrighteousness
Agni: Fire god
Agnistambha: Pillar of fire
Airavata: Indra's vehicle, elephant
Amaravati: Home of Indra
Amavasya: New moon
Anjana: Mother of Aanjaneya/Hanuman
Aanjaneya/Hanuman: God with a monkey body, Rama devotee, helped save Sita from Ravana
Ardhachandra: Crescent moon
Ardhanareeshvara: Combined form of Shiva and Parvati
Ashram: Hermitage
Asura: Children of Brahma and Diti. They live under the ground.
Bhagirath: Sage who brought Ganga to earth
Brahma: Creator of the universe
Brihaspati/Guru: Jupiter, a Navagraha and guru of the gods
Budha: Mercury, a Navagraha
Chaitratha: Kubera's garden
Chandra: Moon, a Navagraha
Chitragupta: Record keeper of human deeds, assists Yama
Daanava: Children of Danu
Deva: Children of Brahma and Aditi. They live above the ground.
Dhanvantari: Celestial doctor
Dikpaala: Guardian
Dyaus/Akasha: Ether
Ganga: Holy river
Garuda: Vishnu's vehicle
Halaahala: Poison that emerged from Samudramanthana
Hanuman: Rama's devotee, god with a monkey body who helped rescue Sita from Lanka
Harihara: Harihara is the combined form of Vishnu and Shiva
Indra: Rain god, king of gods
Ishana: Form of Shiva, guardian of the northeast
Kailasa: Mountain on which Shiva and Parvati live
Ketu: A Navagraha
Kheer: rice pudding
Krishna Paksha: Period between the full moon and the new moon
Kubera: God of riches
Kumbhakarana: Ravana's younger
Lakshmi: Goddess of wealth, prosperity and abundance
Linga: An elongated semi-ellipsoid stone representation of Shiva
Loka: World (there are a total of 14)

Mahabharata: Epic that tells the story of the Pandavas and Kauravas
Mangal: Planet Mars, a Navagraha
Manu: Father of the human race
Naga: Cobra
Nairiti: Goddess of darkness, calamity, sorrow, guardian of the southwest
Nakshatra: Lunar mansions, distinct segments of the sky through which the Moon travels during its monthly cycle. Each nakshatra possesses unique characteristics and influences
Nara: Human male
Narada: Sage
Naravaahana: Another name of Kubera
Nari: Human female
Navagraha: Nine gods of Hindu astrology
Parikrama: Circumambulation
Paataala Loka: One of the lokas
Pitraloka: Home of Yama
Poornima: night of full moon
Prithvi / Bhumi: earth
Pushpak: self-propelling ariel vehicle
Radha: Form of Lakshmi, lover of Krishna
Rahu: A Navagraha
Rama: Avatar of Vishnu, hero of Ramayana
Ramayana: Epic narrating story of Rama. Written in Sanskrit by Valmiki
Ravana: King of Lanka
Rishi: Enlightened person
Samudra: Sea/oceans
Samudramanthana: Churning of the ocean
Sanjana/Sharanya: Surya's wife
Saraswati: Goddess of knowledge, speech and learning
Shani: Saturn, a Navagraha
Shankha: Conch
Shatarupa: Mother of the human race
Sheshanaag: the King of Nagas (serpents), supports earth upon his thousand hoods, serves as the bed of Vishnu
Shiva: God of destruction
Shukla Paksha: Period of waxing moon, when the moon gets bigger in size
Shukra: Venus, a Navagraha
Sita: Form of Lakshmi, daughter of earth, wife of Rama
Soma rasa: juice of the Soma plant, invigorating drink may have intoxicating effect
Sriramacharitamanasa: Epic narrating story of Rama in Awadhi (dialect of Hindi) by Tulsidas
Surya: Sun god, a Navagraha
Swayamvara: a ceremony for choosing a husband

Tathaastu: Sanskrit word meaning 'so be it'
Tika/Tilak: Auspicious mark at the centre of the eyebrows
Vaahana: Vehicle
Vaanara: Not human, often associated with monkeys
Vaikuntha: The home of Vishnu and Lakshmi
Vajra: Thunderbolt
Valmiki: Sage, author of Ramayana
Varaaha: Boar, avatar of Vishnu
Vayu: Wind god
Vyasa: Seer, compiler of Rig Veda, Yajur Veda, Sama Veda and Atharva Veda and author of Mahabharata
Vishnu: Protecter of universe
Vishwakarma: Architect, engineer and designer of the gods
Yagna: Any ritual done in front of a sacred fire, often with mantras
Yali: a creature with the head and body of a lion, the trunk and tusks of an elephant, and occasionally features of a horse
Yama: God of the dead, lord of justice, dikpaala of the south
Yamaloka: Home of Yama
Yami/Yamuna: River, sister of Yama
Yoga: A spiritual and physical discipline widely practised for health and relaxation
Yuga: An age of humankind

SELECT READING

Barnett, Lionel D. *Hindu Gods and Heroes: Studies in the History of the Religion of India*. E P Dutton and Company, 1922.
Frazer, James G. *The Worship of Nature*. Macmillan & Co, 1926.
Pillai, Vidvan G. *Tree-worship and Ophiolatry*. Annamalai University Publication, 1948.
Puri, Usha. *Bhartiya Mithak Kosh*. National Publishing House, 1986.
Rao, K.L. Sheshagiri, and Kapil Kapoor, editors. *Encyclopedia of Hinduism*. Rupa & Co, 2012.
Srivastava, Snehlata. *Gwala Bhaiya*. Sasta Sahitya Mandal, 2011.
Verma, Dheera. *Siddhartha*. Sasta Sahitya Mandal, 2011.
Verma, Sunanda. *Namaste, Bindeshwar Pathak!* Indologist, 2020.
Verma, Vimlesh K. *Ab Chita Cheta Chiitrakutahin Chal*. Centre of Cultural Resource and Training, Ministry of Culture, Govt. of India, 2022.
Verma, Vimlesh K. *Bhartenduyugin Hindi Kavya Mein Lok Tatwa*. Rishabh Charan Jain & Santati, 1964.
Verma, Vimlesh K. *Ganga*. Dreamland Publications, 2001.
Verma, Vimlesh K., and Sunanda V. Asthana. *Learner's Hindi English Thematic Visual Dictionary*. Sasta Sahitya Mandal, 2013.
Verma, Vimlesh K., and Sunanda Verma. *Index of Sriramacaritamanasa* by Goswami Tulasidasa. IGNCA, Ministry of Culture, Govt. of India, 2024.
Vidyalankar, Satyakam. *The Holy Vedas: A Golden Treasury*. Clarion Books, 1983.
Walker, Barbara G. *The Woman's Dictionary of Symbols and Sacred Objects*. HarperCollins, 1988.
Ward, William. *A View of the History, Literature, and Religion of the Hindoos: Including a Minute Description of Their Manners and Customs, and Translations from Their Principal Works*. 5th ed., Mission Press, 1818.
Wilkins, William J. Hindu Mythology, *Vedic and Purānic*. Thacker, Spink & Co, 1882.
Wundt, Wilhelm. *Elements of Folk Psychology—Outline of a Psychological History of the Development of Mankind*. George Allen & Unwin Ltd, 2008.

ACKNOWLEDGEMENTS

I don't know what I might be born as in my next life, but I believe I must have done well in my previous ones to have people who support me in ways that makes me see the divine in them!

Thank you, dear friend and publisher Vidhi Bhargava for trusting me with *Hindu Gods and Goddesses* and believing in its depth and scope. Your faith has been my fuel.

Thank you, Seetha Natesh for your careful editing and insightful suggestions.

Thank you, Aparajitha Vaasudev for interpreting the text with intuition and giving it form and colour through your art.

Thank you, Papa, Dr Vimlesh Kanti Verma. Your wisdom, guidance and patience are Shakti, from where everything begins. You are the guru everyone needs.

Thank you, dada, Dr Sunoor Verma for being Shiva and Hanuman, pushing me towards challenging tasks and supporting me with perspectives.

Thank you, Anshuman for being Vishwakarma and Vishnu, helping me craft my thoughts through discussions and happily ensuring that our life together is sustainable.

Thank you, Avi and Viti for being Surya and bringing light and warmth, day after day.

Memories of two incredible storytellers, Buaji, Dr Snehlata Srivastava and Amma, Dheera Verma and their stories, strengthen me every day. They are not here to hold this book today but I know will be happy to see their stories here and to know that every story made a difference.